To: Pa
We
you, we thank God
for sending you to us.
Love,
Dr. Ray

NESTLE
OR
WRESTLE

The Choice Is Yours

Dr. Barbara Ray

NESTLE OR WRESTLE

The Choice Is Yours

Dr. Barbara Ray

Scriptures quotations are from:
The Holy Bible, New International Version. Copyright 1973, 1984 by International Bible Society. Used by permission of Zondervan Publishing House. All rights reserved.

New American Standard Bible Copyright 1960, 1977, 1995 by the Lockman Foundation. Used by permission.

The Holy Bible, New King James Version (NKJV) Copyright by Thomas Nelson, Inc.

PUBLISHED BY:
BRENTWOOD CHRISTIAN PRESS
4000 BEALLWOOD AVENUE
COLUMBUS, GEORGIA 31904

This book is dedicated to our two precious children,
Renee' Cotton, and Rodney Ray and to our
wonderful son-in-law, Bill Cotton, to our wonderful
daughter-in-law, Julia Ray, and to our precious
grandchildren; Mandy Cotton, Brady Cotton,
Evelyn Ray, Jones Ray, and Parker Ray.
We love them all dearly and nestle them
in our hearts every day.

ACKNOWLEDGMENTS

First and foremost, I would like to say a very special thank you to my husband, Jesse Ray, for being that special person who loves me and inspires me to go beyond what I think I am capable of doing. My love for him has grown and continues to grow as we walk together in the paths that God chooses for us. Darling, you are my love and I look forward to many more years of nestling together.

Thanks also to Justin Fennell for encouraging me to write this book and for guiding me along the way. A special thanks to you for having faith in me.

I would also like to acknowledge Brentwood Christian Press for their help. Thank you for being so cheerful and congenial in response to all my inquiries.

And finally, a special thank you to the many dear people who, through the years, have trusted me enough to share their lives with me. I am sincerely humbled by your trust in me.

INTRODUCTION

My son called me so excited over his decision to go, with a group of his friends, snow skiing in Aspen, Colorado. This was my son's first time to ski and like any mother I was a little worried about his safety. I did not want to ruin the thrill of his trip by expressing my fears but I did feel free to ask a (dumb) mother question. I asked him if they would teach him how to ski before he got on the slopes. I knew when he answered, "Oh mother," that it was not a very smart question. He explained to me that he would have to spend the first day in a ski class being instructed on how to ski correctly. After a day of being shown how to ski he would then be allowed on the slopes. He assured me that they would teach him everything he needed to know in order to be safe.

Needless to say I was very happy when my son returned from his trip with no broken bones. He was still excited and said he planned to go snow skiing again the next year. He said being taught what to do in class made learning to ski on the slopes so much easier and after the initial fear, he began to really enjoy skiing down the steep slopes. The key to his enjoyment was being shown how to ski by someone who had spent a lifetime on the slopes. He would have had a much tougher time and maybe a few broken bones if he had tried to learn to ski on his own.

There is nothing like being shown how to do something by someone who has knowledge and experience in doing the very thing you are trying to do. You benefit from what they have learned, perhaps many times, through trial and error. Just as instruction by a qualified instructor is valuable in recreational sports, it is just that valuable in other areas of life. This is especially true in the area of marriage. That is the reason I want to share with you the knowledge and experience I have gleaned from: (1) being married fifty years, (2) counseling hundreds of couples and (3) teaching Marriage and Family courses.

Another reason I want to share my knowledge about marriage with you is because of a note written by one of my students, a young lady in my Marriage and Family class. She wrote a note on her evaluation form sincerely thanking me for giving the class hope that marriages really could last. She said that prior to that class she had felt that marriage in general, was doomed. I was glad that I had given her and the class hope and that is what I want to give you - hope! Hope – faith that your marriage will last for a lifetime.

Ministers, psychologists, sociologists, marriage counselors, have all contributed to the vast knowledge we have concerning marriage. All of these professionals along with the articles that have been written, the seminars that have been conducted and the marriage encounters that have been attended have helped countless couples have the marriage they so desperately wanted. I am very thankful for all of these dedicated people who have given so much to help marriage be what it was intended to be. And now I would like to ask you to consider this my personal instruction book written with the desire to help you and your spouse avoid the falls that will result in a broken relationship.

Unlike the ski instructors, that helped my son, I can't be there with you physically but as you read this book please know that I am with you in spirit. I have entitled the book, *"Nestle or Wrestle"* because having personally experienced both "wrestling" and "nestling" in our marriage, my husband and I want the record to show that "nestling" is so much more enjoyable and satisfying than "wrestling."

I believe it is possible to nestle and to show someone that they are nestled in many ways. In the marriage relationship the way we want to nestle or be nestled changes over time, because we change, situations change, and our needs change. However, in each stage of marriage the need to be nestled is there. We just have to care enough to learn the best way to nestle at any given time. Remember, when we nestle we not only bring love but comfort and security to our marriage.

It is my prayer that the simplicity of this book will encourage you and your spouse to strive for that close and loving relationship, spending valuable time nestling each other through the good times as well as those times when things get pretty rough. Life will not always go as you would like it but remember:

Ecclesiastes 4:9-12
9 Two are better than one,
because they have a good return for their work:
10 If one falls down,
his friend can help him up.
But pity the man who falls
and has no one to help him up!
11 Also, if two lie down together, they will keep warm.
But how can one keep warm alone?
12 Though one may be overpowered,
two can defend themselves.
A cord of three strands is not quickly broken.

You have undertaken this wonderful adventure together and however rough it gets just hold tight to each other (nestle) and you will make it.

7

CONTENTS

1

THE NEED TO BE CLOSE

From the moment of birth a baby desires to be touched by another human being. There is something about being held close and cradled in loving arms that soothes and comforts like nothing else. This need to be touched and held close is something that we never outgrow. As adults we still have a need to be close to someone, to be physically and emotionally connected to another person. But reality tells us that this does not always happen for we have all heard stories of those who feel so disconnected and totally alone that they give up on life.

It is hard to believe that in a world so full of people that there are those who feel completely alone. Loneliness and disconnectedness are big problems. The issue of being connected to others has been written about in many popular magazines and it seems that newspaper advice columnists are constantly answering letters from people who say they have no one that they feel close to. It is sad to think that many people may surround those who are lonely but still they feel isolated and alone. It is even sadder to think that some of those who are so lonely are sharing their lives with another person; they are married and yet they feel very alone and lonely.

The thought of people being so lonely bothers me but what bothers me more is the thought that those who are married feel so alone. Being married to someone should mean that a person has someone with whom they really feel connected. Marriage should be a place of nestling, being held close by someone you love.

It is true that marriage itself does not insure that we will never experience loneliness again, but a good marriage does give us the comfort of being connected to another human being. Of all relationships that we might have, it is the marriage relationship that should give us the assurance that we have someone close who will always be there for us. This assurance helps to banish loneliness because we know that we are held affectionately close in the other's heart even when we are unable to physically hold each other. This kind of closeness is inspired and motivated by love and it is something that we all yearn for.

Families that Prepare Us to Nestle

The need to be held close really begins at the moment of birth and continues throughout our lives. Many of us were fortunate to grow up in families, which even though they were not perfect, were close and loving. We felt that love and closeness during good times and bad times. As a parent, I remember when our children were going through rough times and I held them close in my heart and many times nestled them in my arms. Those are such comforting memories for me and I am sure for them as well.

Being close to someone we love stirs up all kinds of emotions within us. We experience feelings of love, excitement, contentment, and security. We can experience these feelings when we hold those we love physically close, but we can also experience these same feelings when we hold those we love emotionally close. To be so connected to

10

another person gives us the energy and stamina we need to face life. This connectedness and closeness not only brings us comfort but it is also good for our physical and emotional well-being.

A Childhood Memory

I am reminded of the times in my life when things seemed pretty sad and someone who loved me held me affectionately close. Somehow being held close seemed to ease the hurt. I knew I was loved and that made me less vulnerable. I am sure we can all think of times when just being held in someone's arms helped us face life with fewer misgivings.

A special memory for me happened when I was in the Third Grade. The teacher that year was especially cruel, not only to me but also to the other students in her class. On one particular day I became the target of her cruelty. I was just getting over a cold and was able to be in school but I still had a dry cough. We were in the middle of a lesson and I coughed. The teacher warned me, in a stern voice, not to do that again. I was mortified. I was always a good student and I could not believe that I had been reprimanded so sternly for something that I could not help. I tried desperately not to cough but eventually I coughed again.

The teacher reminded me that I had been warned not to do that and if I did that again she would paddle me. I held my throat and even tried not to breathe, but eventually I coughed again. She had me come to the front of the room and get her ruler out of her desk. In front of the entire class she paddled my hand and said to me "Do not ever cough again without putting your hand over your mouth." She had never mentioned putting my hand over my mouth. I thought she had been warning me not to cough again.

11

I cried the rest of the day at school and all the way home. When I got home I immediately told my mother what had happened at school. She was angry and determined to pay my teacher a visit. I began to plead with her not to go to the school for a talk with my teacher. After much pleading on my part she eased my fears and said she would not go. My mother then took me in her arms and rocked me and held me affectionately close. I will never forget the love I felt from my mother as she held me close and comforted me.

Most of us can remember the times when we were made to feel sad because someone hurt our feelings. Somehow just a hug or a comforting word made us feel all wrapped up in love and the pain of the moment did not seem quite so bad. This kind of loving closeness gives us the kind of start that makes life easier to handle. The loving closeness we experience with our family is something to be valued.

Through the adolescent years, and into early adulthood, we establish close relationships with our friends. There is nothing like having best friends with whom to share our secrets. Really good friends are our friends for life. As the years go by, miles may separate us, but there is always that special place in our hearts for our best friends. These friendships are so rewarding because of the closeness we feel with each other. Throughout the years we can and do hold our friends close in our hearts.

Someone Special

Sometime in early adulthood we start looking for a different kind of close relationship. A relationship that is different than what we have with our parents or our friends. What we are really yearning for is someone special with whom we can share a closeness that we have never experienced before. We want to experience a closeness that comes with a special kind of love relationship. Most of us begin to look for this special kind of love in early adulthood. Some are bolder than others in their attempt to find someone they can share their love and life with. Others just sort of wait and let it happen. However, when we feel this special love, we know it!

I personally have a problem with the term "falling in love." I don't think we fall in love; it is more like we grow in love. There may be that initial excitement that we feel when our chemistry is stirred by the presence of that certain person, but love goes much deeper than that. True love comes as you get to really know each other and I like to think, become friends.

Many couples often wonder if they have found their true love - the one they want to marry. How will they know when they are really in love? This morning I heard a TV personality say that when you find the right person to marry you will know it. He said, "You will know, you will just know." I agree; you will know.

It is amazing what happens when we really know that we are in love. For one thing, we find ourselves constantly thinking about the one we love and how much we want to be with him or her.

I remember when my husband and I first knew that we were in love; every moment together was like a little bit of heaven. When we were together he didn't want to leave and I didn't want him to leave. We loved being close to each other. My husband loves to tell our friends how, when we were dating, he would call me on the phone several times a day just to hear me breathe. We felt so close we just knew that we were really soul mates.

When we find that special someone we begin to enjoy an emotional closeness we have never experienced. We also begin to look forward to the physical closeness that makes marriage so special. We think about how wonderful it will be to spend the rest of our lives being together and holding each other close. We are anxious to marry and to make a commitment to love, honor and cherish. After marriage we know we can hold each other close emotionally and physically as long as we live.

When we become husband and wife most of us feel deliriously happy - we are finally married. We know that for the rest of our lives we will be in love - we will always be close! There will always be love in the morning, love at noontime, and love when the sun goes down. Then reality hits! "My husband used to say that the honey gives out and the moon goes down." I say, "Hang in there, the honey can be replenished and the moon will rise again."

A Choice Has to be Made

In the real world we have to put forth a lot of effort to have a close and loving marriage. There are problems to work through and things do not always go as smoothly as we thought they would. But thank the Lord, we discover it is possible for two people who <u>choose</u> to love, to stay close to each other spiritually, emotionally, and physically. Trust me when I say it is possible to have a great marriage. God planned marriage to be the best and most satisfying relationship that a man and woman can have on this earth. Why not go for the best – being friends, lovers, and soul mates for life. Enjoy a marriage that has more nestling than wrestling – the choice is yours. Hopefully the following chapters of this book will give you some insight into what it takes to have this kind of relationship.

2

BY GOD'S DESIGN

The great news for all of us is that God, not some modern day marriage guru, designed marriage. Knowing that God was and is concerned about His creation, we have to know that He established marriage for our pleasure and fulfillment. In the beginning God saw that the man He had created needed someone of his own kind so God created Eve for Adam. Read this part of the creation story in *Genesis 2,* and rejoice over the fact that Adam was elated with the woman that God had made for him. She belonged to him for she was part of him.

Genesis 2:21-23

21   So the LORD God caused a deep sleep to fall upon the man, and he slept; then He took one of his ribs, and closed up the flesh at that place.

22   And the LORD God fashioned into a woman the rib which He had taken from the man, and brought her to the man.

And the man said, "This is now bone of my bones, and flesh of my flesh; she shall be called woman, because she was taken out of Man."

Therefore shall a man leave his father and his mother, and shall cleave unto his wife: and they shall be one flesh.

Talk about closeness! God made the woman and brought her to the man and said that the two should be as one. This is such a beautiful picture of the closeness a husband and wife can enjoy. The thought of such spiritual, emotional, and physical closeness is exhilarating. We become so close we are as "one." It can't get much better than that. This is what we want when get married, we want to be close and stay close to the person God has given us to love and cherish.

Include the Designer

Since God designed marriage in the first place don't you think it is wise to include Him in marriage today? It is risky to try to make a marriage work without including the designer. When a couple includes God in their marriage it stands a much better chance of being a good marriage. Look at it this way, when the personal relationship is right vertically (with God) it is much easier to keep the horizontal relationship (with your spouse) as it should be. It takes a lot of work and a lot of prayer to have a good marriage.

The first few years of our marriage were very difficult and without God's help we would not have made it. We each had a personal relationship with God, which helped us to hold steady during the stormy times. I'm sure we both had to do a lot of praying. Believe it or not, on occasions I even had to ask God to give me love for my husband. Many times I asked God to let His love for my husband flow through me. I knew God loved him and at times I didn't know whether I did or not. I am sure my husband had to pray the same way regarding his love for me. We know, from personal experience that God must be included in the marriage if it is going to be all you want it to be.

Psalm 127:1
Unless the LORD builds the house, they labor in vain who build it; unless the LORD guards the city, the watchman keeps awake in vain.

The Lord is the master builder and asking His guidance in building your lives together is the most important thing you can do. When those trouble times come in your marriage, and they will come, you will know that you have the Lord to help you.

You see, during the dating years we all envision what it will be like when we find and marry the person we want to spend the rest of our lives with. We have great expectations of how life is going to be once we get married. We envision days of basking in each other's love because we know that the fire of romance will always be a part of our relationship. Unlike other married couples we have known, we know that we will always be blissfully happy.

Unrealistic Expectation

As my fiancée and I approached our wedding date I had all those unrealistic expectations and I knew all of my dreams about marriage were about to come true. We were both Christians so I expected to live in marital bliss everyday. I thought as Christians we would always see eye to eye on everything and that we would never have any arguments. That theory was blown in just a short few weeks. I found that there were many things about which we disagreed. At times, the arguments became very heated. I would cry and he would leave. Yes, there were times when he even slept on the couch. And we were Christians!

I felt so guilty because I thought that this should not be happening to us, we should not be having marital problems. I failed to understand that when two people, from different backgrounds, begin to live in the same house day after day it is very unlikely that they will agree on everything. In the early years of our marriage when we would have a disagreement we would end up in a heated argument with a lot of hurtful things being said. It took us a while to learn it was much better to allow each other to say what we had to say without the other getting angry. With a lot of work and a great deal of patience we finally learned that getting so angry did not accomplish anything.

I must tell you that having the freedom to say how we honestly felt about something really helped us appreciate each other more. After all, home is a place we should feel free to give our opinion or say how we feel without fear of repercussion. However, a word of caution is needed here, opinions and feelings should be expressed in a kind and loving way. Stating your opinion about something in order to hurt or "put down" your spouse does a lot of damage to the marriage.

A Word of Encouragement

Let me offer a word of encouragement; if you and your spouse both love the Lord but are still having difficulties in your marriage, take heart. You have the privilege of asking God to help you work through those difficult times and He can, and will, help you. Many couples that have had long and happy marriages will tell you *"God is a very present help in the time of trouble..."* Prayer and trust in God has helped many marriages survive the storms of marital difficulties.

Offense versus Defense

The work on having a close relationship in marriage begins before marriage. I can almost hear some of you saying, "We had no problem being close UNTIL we got married and then everything changed." This does happen, but it does not happen without a reason. It happens because two people, who say they love each other, did not bother to look close enough at their marriage to find out what happened to cause them to drift apart.

In years of doing pre-marital counseling I have seen the adoring looks passing between young couples as they shared their stories of love with me. Young love is such a thrilling thing to observe and there is always the hope that such love will grow stronger and will last a lifetime. It is sad to say that some of the couples who appeared to be so much in love before marriage would, after a few months, come back to see me because their marriage was in trouble. The loving words and adoring looks that had been such a part of their relationship before were now noticeably absent. In fact, most of those couples that came back to see me with marital problems would not even look at each other or express any affection whatsoever.

As a distraught couple would sit before me, I could not help but think how very much in love they had been just a short time ago. They seemed to be so close and now, as they sit in my office, they appear very indifferent to each other. I could sense no closeness whatever in their relationship, now they appeared to be two strangers sitting side by side. Of course each was blaming the other for their difficulties.

Some couples find themselves in this situation after being married just a short time while others stay in a relationship that is void of any emotional closeness for many years. Any couple living without the emotional closeness that God intended for marriage is unhappy in their relationship, no matter how long they have been married.

Something has to happen for a couple to reach a place in their marriage where they feel totally disconnected. Whether it was a one-time incident or an unresolved issue, they did not deal with it in a positive way. In every marriage, even in good marriages, there will be disagreements but it is during these times of disagreements that adjustments and compromises have to be, or need to be, made.

In my years of counseling I have seen couples that have been married for fifteen, twenty and sometimes thirty years, who are so unhappy in their marriage. Many would tell me that if things were not going to get any better they wanted out of the marriage. It was very sad to me to see two people who had invested so much of their lives into a marriage to get to the place where they saw no hope for their future together.

Maybe some of you who are reading this book feel there is no hope for your marriage. Please don't give up; something may change if you do what you alone can do and perhaps your situation will improve. You cannot change another person's behavior but you can change your attitude toward that behavior and maybe the other person will change in response to your changed attitude.

Marriage is an Adventure

The words of an old song go something like this, "If you ever needed the Lord before, you sure do need Him now." How true! Entering into marriage is like going on an adventure, which we are told, involves danger and the unknown. Pre-marital counseling is certainly beneficial and I like to say, necessary. However, whether you did or did not have pre-marital counseling, rest assured that a few surprises await you as you begin and continue this marriage adventure.

Marriage as an adventure is a very exciting and sometimes risky experience. If you are just beginning this marriage adventure I want to offer a word of encouragement as someone who has already experienced some of the hazards that you may encounter. I offer help also as someone who has studied and taught about marriage for many years. I want to be of help to you by pointing out certain areas where extra precaution and effort are needed. If you have been married a few years I trust that some of what is written will enlighten you as to how you can have a better marriage and an even closer relationship.

The marriage adventure begins with understanding why you and your spouse are the persons you are today. Marriage also begins with understanding why you and your spouse are so totally different in the way you see the marriage relationship and experience life.

3

DELIGHTFUL TRUTH AND DISTRESSFUL REALITY

It is quite possible that after you have been married a short while you awaken to the fact that you don't really know the person you married. You may have known each other all your lives and have dated each other for years, and now all of a sudden you discover you are married to a very strange person. You wonder what happened to the person you knew, loved, and promised to spend the rest of your life with. Nothing has happened, you have just taken off the rose colored glasses and now it is reality time.

A Mistake?

At this stage of your marriage you may feel that you have honestly made a mistake, you surely married the wrong person. It will make you feel somewhat better to know that many people, at this point in their marriage, have felt just as you do. Most of the time it is not that you have married the wrong person, the fact is you are just beginning to see how the person you married lives life. This experience can be a real shocker and at times, not so pleasant. The important thing you need to remember is that with a lot of patience and the passing of time you will adjust to each other's "weird ways."

The very thing that makes the marriage relationship so wonderful can also make you withdraw from each other. You are so different in the way you feel, think, and in general, look at life. At times it is difficult to stay as close as you would like to your spouse because the two of you are so very different. Not only do you look different (thank the Lord) but you also think, talk, and respond differently to just about everything. This can cause some real problems unless you come to understand that your differences are really blessings in disguise. You start by recognizing that God made two different genders: male and female.

Different from Conception

In other words, God made you different from each other in many ways and for some of the differences I am sure you are very grateful. However, we all need help in understanding the differences that are not so easily tolerated. It helps to remember that God made male and female and He designed them so they would be different biologically, physically, emotionally, and psychologically.

I don't want to give you a lesson in biology but I will point out just a few differences between male and female that seem to make life interesting and at times, frustrating. Please know that all the statements I make about differences in males and females are generalizations. In other words, what is said about the differences may not be true for every individual. Understanding that there are some exceptions, let's look at some of the differences between the sexes.

To begin, we know that both male and female share the same hormones but in varying amounts. The male has a higher level of the testosterone hormone whereas the female has more of the hormone, estrogen. These hormones account for some of the differences in how we look, think, feel, and behave. Males are more aggressive and females more emotional. When I say that women are more emotional, men are quick to agree and they usually give me a hearty AMEN! It appears to be very difficult for men to understand how women can be so emotional, especially during certain times of the month.

Roller Coaster Emotions are not easy to Deal With

In teaching Marriage and Family classes, young men often asked me, "What can I do when my wife is experiencing PMS and her emotions have gone hay wire?" "When I try to hold her, she says leave me alone, when I leave her alone, she says I don't care about her." "What can I do?" I would tell them, "do the best you can - hold her until she says no and let go when she says let go. Let her vent her emotions (to a reasonable degree) in the safe environment of your love" To be honest, that is the same thing I would tell husbands today as well.

I had one young man tell me, "When my wife is in her pre-menstrual cycle she is mean, she is really mean!" I could not help but laugh. I did feel sorry for him and I also felt sorry for his wife. I am sure that she did not want to be mean, she just couldn't help herself. I used to tell my husband that I would feel better if I could bite a nail. That sounds a little strange but it expressed exactly how I felt at the time.

It is all about hormones. Things that would not normally bother a woman will bother her at this time. There are a lot of symptoms connected with PMS but the psychological symptoms seem to cause the most trouble for the husband. Husbands, it is well to remember that she is depressed, irritable, and she feels fat and ugly.

There are things that can be done to help PMS, such as diet, exercise and taking certain vitamins. The big news is the medical world finally listened and recognized that PMS is real. Now they have medicine that can be taken to help with some of the mood swings, hooray! Another big help for a woman who is suffering from PMS is the support of her husband and family. So husband be kind to yourself and to your wife and see that she gets what she needs to help her deal with her fluctuating hormones.

Some Differences may be seen as Assets

There are physical differences between the male and female that we, at times, may consider assets. Men have greater brute strength, thicker skulls, and wider shoulders. The man's greater strength and wider shoulders are assets to him in performing heavy tasks around the house or on a job. This is also good since men have traditionally been expected to carry the financial burden of providing for the physical needs of their families. The greater strength of the male is to be appreciated.

We are told that women have more enduring strength and wider hips. Most women feel that their enduring strength is an asset, something they need in caring for the needs of their family. In marriage seminars I use as an example of enduring strength the ability of a woman (wife and/or mother) to keep working regardless of how she feels physically. A wife will somehow manage to take care of husband and family when she is sick enough that she should be in bed.

We will now examine whether or not we can consider the wider hips a blessing. It is suggested that the wider hips make it easier for a woman to carry her unborn child during pregnancy; that is a blessing. However, some women do not consider wider hips an asset but something they are plagued with all their lives. Wider hips are not a problem for some women but for others it is definitely a problem.

In seminars, when I mention that the male has a thicker skull the ladies always laugh and remark, "That is why my husband never hears what I tell him, he is too thick headed." To be fair to the men and to give them a laugh as well, I tell them that some researchers say that the female's lip muscles are moving at birth. The men like that and usually say, "Their lips were moving at birth and they have never stopped." They go on to say that their wives talk so much they just tune them out. After all, turn about is fair play; I want to be fair to both.

She Personalizes

Another difference is that females tend to personalize whatever they are sensing and feeling, whereas; males tend to project what they sense or feel. This difference can, at times, be frustrating. I am well aware of the female's tendency to personalize but on occasions I still find myself personalizing statements my husband makes about someone.

Just the other day my husband mentioned that a certain lady seemed to be gaining weight. I immediately started thinking that he might think I was gaining weight also. If I had said to him what I was thinking (I have done this) he would have been very aggravated with me. He probably would have told me how ridiculous it was of me to think he was even insinuating that I was gaining weight. Personalizing things can cause a lot of frustration, so it is best to try not to personalize. I am honestly going to try. Sorry, it is a female thing!

He Projects

To be fair it is just as frustrating for a husband to project his feelings. For instance, a husband feeling guilty about not helping out around the house might say to his wife that she doesn't appreciate what he does for her. He goes on to emphasize the fact that he goes to work everyday and provides well for his family and that is more than some men do. He wants his wife to feel guilty for expecting him to help around the house. He is trying to project the guilt he feels on to his wife. Sorry, it is a male thing!

Interesting but Humorous

A difference that I find quite interesting is the ability of the female to read facial expressions somewhat better than the male. A woman can respond immediately to what she is sensing by the facial expression of another. Many times because of her ability to read facial expressions, a wife can save the day.

Picture this - two couples are standing in front of a church chatting with each other. On the spur of the moment one of the husbands invites the other couple over for lunch. The husband of the couple who has just been invited, without hesitation says, "That is a great idea; sure we would love to go." The wife of the husband, who did the inviting, is thinking of what her home looks like; the unmade beds, the dirty dishes, and the clothes all over the floor. She is horror stricken, but she puts on a smile and meekly nods her head in agreement. However, the wife of the husband who has accepted the invitation sees and reads the facial expression of the other wife. She understands and she persuades her husband to decline. As the couples leave, a sigh of relief escapes the lips of both wives. An embarrassing situation avoided as a result of the ability of a wife to read a facial expression that somehow escaped her husband's notice.

Equal in Intellectual Ability

I am happy to say that, according to research, males and females have the same intellectual ability and neither should look at the other as being inferior. However, there is a tendency to think that our partner is intellectually inferior when he or she sees things differently than the way we see them. Many times this difference of opinion is a result of looking at a problem from our gender specific perspective. Understanding gender differences is one way you can get to know why your husband/wife thinks or acts the way he/she does.

The Home in Which you were Reared

Another reason you think and act differently is that you have different backgrounds. It helps to understand that you and your spouse are who you are, in part, as a result of the family to which you were born and reared. If you and your spouse lived as next-door neighbors, you were still reared differently. For what went on behind the doors of your house is what made you what you are as a person.

The physical and emotional environment in your home, from the time you were born, influenced your likes, dislikes, habits, and your self-esteem. Your personality characteristics came not only from your genes (from your mother, father, grandparents, aunts, uncles, etc.) but also from the significant others in your life and how they treated you as you were growing up.

If you were treated well it is likely that you grew up feeling good about who you are. That means you have high self-esteem and a positive self-image, which has helped or will help you to achieve your goals in life. On the other hand, if by some unfortunate circumstances you were treated unfairly you might have low self-esteem and a poor self-image, which, in turn, can cause a lot of negative feelings.

These negative feelings can cause you some problems unless you deal with the issues that have caused you to see yourself in such a poor light. It is possible to come to grips with why you feel as you do and why you see yourself as you do. When you do this, then you can ask God to help you to see yourself as He sees you, a person worthy of love and acceptance.

Get to know who you are, why you feel as you do, and do your best to correct any wrong image and move on. But, please come to terms with any baggage from your past; don't bring it with you into your relationship. If you insist on hauling it with you or using it as a crutch, you are asking for failure. We are all products of our upbringing, but we can choose to focus on the positive and do our best to eliminate the negative.

Different Families – Different Lifestyles

Each family has their own particular lifestyle. Because we were reared in a particular family, we tend to think our own family's lifestyle is the right one. For instance, in my family every Saturday was hamburger day. We didn't have to eat vegetables on that day, and Mother didn't have to cook a big meal. We looked forward to Saturday.

In my husband's family Saturday was no different than any other day, his Mother cooked a full meal as usual. When we were first married, I expected Saturday to be "hamburger day." I felt that I didn't have to cook a regular meal because this was fun day. My husband said, "No way, we didn't eat hamburgers on Saturday, we ate a regular meal." Guess what? I thought my family's Saturday meal was the right way. My husband thought his family's Saturday meal was the right way. Trouble in Raysville!

When I would tell this story to my students in Marriage and Family classes, they would invariably ask, who won? Can you believe that we wrestled with this for quiet a while? We made a big issue out of something as insignificant as what type of meal we would eat on Saturdays. If you let yourself you can be very stubborn and make anything, however small, a big issue.

I think I honestly felt that if we didn't eat hamburgers on Saturday that I was somehow being disloyal to my family and my husband probably felt the same way. We were both pretty stubborn in the way we felt and we each wanted to come out the winner. At this point in our marriage we did not know that there should not be a winner or loser in a marital argument.

When we realized that we didn't want all of our Saturdays to be ruined we finally came to a compromise. Some Saturdays we would eat hamburgers, and some Saturdays I would cook a regular meal, and we were both nice about it. A simple solution but it worked. Saturdays became much more enjoyable and I'm sure we found it much easier to stay close to each other -- to nestle, not wrestle.

That was just one of our little Waterloos, and believe me, there were quite a few others. Other couples have had to compromise because one grew up as a night person, the other as a morning person. One might have grown up always going to the beach for vacation; the other always going to mountains, again compromise is needed. The point to be made here is that we all come into marriage expecting to carry over, into our own homes and families, what we did and how we did it, in the homes in which we were reared. But remember we are talking about two different households and two different ways of doing things.

Try to understand where your spouse is coming from and don't treat him or her as though his or her family's way of doing things was dumb. After all, he or she could feel the same way about your family. You both need to realize that you are combining two totally different backgrounds into one present whole and that takes work. It can be done, and it will be done, with a little time, patience, and a lot of compromising.

Habits that Irritate

Now we come to some little foxes that spoil the vines and might make you want to be anything but close to your spouse. I am talking about those little habits that can irritate and drive you crazy.

A case in point might be a spouse who has a habit of never closing a drawer that he or she has opened. This gets on your nerves after a while. Another scenario might be a spouse who never picks up his/her dirty laundry, but drops it on the floor where he or she took it off. What do you do when you end up with a non-drawer closer or a dirty clothes dropper, or both? You can constantly nag hoping that it will finally have some effect, but to be honest; nagging just doesn't do much good. It is better to find a creative way of dealing with the frustrating habits of a spouse.

Instead of constantly nagging about some annoying habit, try to approach it in a positive way. Think of some really positive trait about your spouse, and then sincerely compliment him or her on that particular trait. Follow the positive statement with how much you would appreciate it if he or she would stop doing whatever it is that irritates you. The key to making this work is if they make even a small adjustment, like closing one drawer out of ten, please notice and praise him or her for doing it. Say, "I see you closed this drawer that makes me so happy." Top it off with a nice hug. Please don't say, "Thank you for closing that one drawer; I'll close the other nine."

Be consistent with your praise for any small step he or she does toward changing an irritating habit. If you happen to be the guilty party, be willing to change. Bad habits can be broken especially when you remember your goal is to create a more peaceful and loving atmosphere in your home. If that means working hard to change or break a habit it is well worth the effort.

It is important to know that male and female differences are also crucial when and where adjustments need to be made in other areas of marriage. Men and women think differently and have a different perspective about family, friends, sex, children, work, finances, and religion. The next chapter will focus on your marriage and the adjustments that might need to be made concerning your family and friends.

4

FIRST PLACE PRIORITY HELPS KEEP ME CLOSE TO YOU

As stated earlier, God should always be first in your life and your relationship with Him takes preeminence over everything else. However, after God, if you are going to have a close and loving relationship in your marriage your spouse has to occupy first place in your life. When you pledge your faith each to the other at your wedding, you are saying from this day forward you are my number one priority.

Leaving and Cleaving

Genesis 2:22-24
22 And the LORD God fashioned into a woman the rib which He had taken from the man, and brought her to the man.
23 And the man said, "This is now bone of my bones, and flesh of my flesh; she shall be called woman, because she was taken out of Man."
24 For this cause a man shall leave his father and his mother, and shall cleave to his wife; and they shall become one flesh.

Cleaving means that you will loyally and unwaveringly adhere or stay close to your spouse. So close that the two of you will become one flesh.

In order to become one flesh and be as close as you would like in your marriage, your spouse must be placed at the top of your priority list, he or she must always be number one with you. His or her needs must come before those of your mother or father, or any other family member. It is just that simple. However, you may find that keeping your spouse in first place is not always an easy thing to do, but it is a necessary thing to do if you want to be happy in your relationship.

After your wedding you probably physically left your parents' home. You may not have moved a long distance away but hopefully you did move out on your own. This is as it should be. At the same time it is also very important that you leave your parents in other ways as well. For instance, you should not depend on them for your physical, emotional, financial or spiritual needs any longer. This type of leaving requires a certain level of maturity and discipline.

A Place for Parents

After marriage you relationship with your parents will be somewhat changed as you become more and more bonded to your spouse. Of course you want continue to show love to your parents as well as to your spouse because you do not want either to feel neglected. Satisfying both your parents and your spouse, at times may be difficult, but if you really want to do the right thing God will guide you in how to "leave and cleave," and still honor and respect your parents.

My husband and I married very young and there were many things that we did not know about establishing relationship priorities. Soon after we were married we found ourselves in a dilemma because neither of us knew how to relate to, or what to do with our in-laws. There were times when I felt my husband put his mother first and times when he would get upset with me because he felt I put my family first. I am sorry to say that the in-laws on both sides did not make it any easier for us. To be honest, we really went through "in-law trauma".

My husband was the oldest of three boys and his mother felt I had taken her son. I, on the other hand, was the baby of the family and my family was very protective of me. It took us several years to sort out just where our families fit into our lives and not a little effort to keep them there.

Having endured the in-law trauma ourselves my husband and I made a promise to each other that we would never interfere in the marriage of our children. Our first child, a daughter, married first and we accepted the young man she married into our family. We kept our promise and we did not and have not to this day interfered with their marriage. They knew if they needed us as a couple, they could call on us.

As in-laws we knew and kept our place in the marriage of our daughter and as a result we have a good relationship with our son-in-law. We were thrilled when he and our daughter gave us our first wonderful granddaughter and grandson. Our son-in-law has been a great husband and Father and we feel blessed to have him as part of our family.

Before our son, who is much younger than our daughter, married, I had taught Marriage and the Family at a State University. I felt I was more knowledgeable regarding in-law relationships, particularly the mother-in-law/ daughter-in-law relationship. I knew, from various studies, that in-law problems are more likely to occur between the boy's mother and her daughter-in-law. I was determined that this

35

was not going to happen in our case, I was going to be a good mother-in-law.

I was teaching my Marriage and Family class about couples and in-laws and the best way to handle different situations. I suggested that it would be a good thing if the prospective bride and the mother of the groom got together prior to the wedding for a heart to heart talk. We discussed how a talk of this nature could help to ease any tension that either might feel. Most of my students, boys and girls, felt a talk like this was a very good idea.

I needed to practice what I taught so I told my future daughter-in-law that I would like for the two of us to enjoy a time alone together. I learned later that she was really frightened over the idea of being alone and having a talk with her future mother-in-law. However, she overcame her fear and we did have our time alone and our heart to heart talk.

I told my sweet future daughter-in-law that from the moment that our son took her as his wife she would have first place in his life. I also told her that if I ever interfered in their marriage to please feel free to tell me. This talk got us off to a very good start and we still have a wonderful relationship today. I love her as a daughter and she and our son have given us another beautiful granddaughter and two handsome grandsons.

My husband and I took the very negative experience that we had with our parents when we first married and made it work for our good. I am sure we have not done everything right but we did allow our daughter and our son to leave us physically and emotionally. It was not easy but we knew that their marriages would have a much better chance of surviving and even flourishing if they learned early on to depend on each other.

When Someone Else Takes First Place

When either spouse puts anyone else in first place, the marriage will never be what it could or should be. Over the years I have seen what can happen when a husband or wife puts someone else first in his or her life. One young couple came to see me with a plea for me to teach them how to have a good marriage. Both husband and wife told me how their own parents' marriage had not been good and neither felt they had been reared in a functional family. They both seemed so sincere in their desire to have a happy marriage and create a healthy atmosphere in which they could raise their children.

However, in the course of counseling this couple, I stated that each had to make the other number one in his or her life. That did not set well with the young wife. Immediately she became irate and said, "My mother will always be number one in my life." I replied very kindly, "You want your marriage to be happy and for this to happen your husband has to have first place in your life." The young wife stood and hit my desk and shouted, "My husband will never have first place, and my Mother will always be number one." When she made that statement I told her that I was sorry, I could not help them have the kind of marriage they had told me they wanted if she was so unwilling to do what I suggested. She angrily stormed out of my office and her young husband looked at me dejectedly and meekly followed her. My heart ached as I envisioned what their future would be like if the young wife did not change her attitude.

On another occasion, a young man declared to me, in the presence of his wife, that as long as his mother lived they would eat lunch at her house every Sunday. The young wife meekly stated that there were times that she would love to stay at home and just the two of them enjoy a Sunday lunch together. Her husband was adamant in his attitude toward always eating every Sunday at his mother's home. In fact, he made it very clear to me that his mother and her feelings took priority over his wife.

The wife then related how she and her husband would pick his mother up for church and her mother-in-law would be allowed to sit in the front seat while she, his wife, would be told to get in the back seat. The young man's mother was neither old nor handicapped so it was not necessary that she occupy the front seat. To make matters worse the young wife, in the presence of her husband, told me that on the drive to church her husband and his mother would talk negatively about her while she sat listening in the back seat. Needless to say I was blown away by the attitude of this young husband and even though I suggested several things that would help he was determined not to make any changes.

I was not surprised when some time later the wife called me long distance to tell me that she and her husband had separated. She said she could not take his lack of concern for her and her feelings any longer. Her longing for a close and loving relationship with her husband had been destroyed by the relationship that he had with his mother.

Granted, the two examples that I have given may be a little extreme but in-laws can, and sometimes do, present a real problem. There are plenty of good in-laws who find and keep their place when their son or daughter gets married, but there are a few that can cause havoc for a daughter-in-law or son-in-law.

No Comparisons

As mentioned earlier, usually if there is trouble with an in-law it is with the husband's mother. One of the causes for a mother-in-law to have problems with a daughter-in-law is that she feels that this young lady has taken her place in her son's life. There is role conflict. The mother has been accustomed to taking care of her son's needs, and all of a sudden someone else is doing her job. It is very hard for some mothers to relinquish the nurturing role and it can create problems for her daughter-in-law.

Husbands, you can help your wife by letting her know what a good job she is doing in meeting your needs. Please don't be guilty of comparing her ability to cook, clean, etc., with how your Mother did it. Remember that your Mother has years of experience and given a little time and encouragement from you, your wife will make you proud.

Sometimes a father is so protective of his daughter that it is hard for him to let go. If she is really dependent on him, she also finds it hard to trust her husband as she has her father. The husband might see this if the wife openly says, "I'll call Daddy, he can fix anything." Wives, please be careful not to make your husbands feel inadequate by implying that they are not able to "fix anything." Show your trust in your husband by making him feel he can do anything. This will build his confidence and he may even surprise you at what he is capable of doing. Showing that you trust him will also keep him from resenting your father.

Stand On Your Own Financially

There are times when your parents or in-laws might use finances as a means of control. You might need some financial help during the early years of marriage, but as soon as possible you should try to make it on your own. Don't become so obligated to your parents financially that they can use it as a means of control. The saying is "there can be no cleaving without leaving." This is not just speaking of leaving physically but also emotionally and financially.

A Couple Problem

It also helps to remember that an in-law problem is not between individuals, it is a couple problem. In other words, if it is between a mother-in-law and a daughter-law, it is still a couple problem. If it is between a father-in-law and a son-in-law, it is still a couple problem. It should always be dealt with as a couple. You go, as a couple, to the person with whom there is difficulty and you talk things out; a husband standing with his wife, and a wife standing with her husband. Be kind and respectful but also firm.

Another good thing for both of you to remember is that what goes on in the husband and wife relationship should be kept between the two of you. When you have a disagreement do not run to mother or daddy and tell on your spouse. If you feel like you have to tell somebody, tell the Lord. He sees both sides and He loves you both. When you tell your parents they have a hard time forgetting and forgiving the spouse that caused suffering for their son or daughter. As husband and wife you will get over it much quicker than your parents so keep your problems and difficulties to yourselves.

At times, in-laws, even though they are adults, can be very childish. They will try to make you feel guilty about not calling or coming by as often as they think you should. Don't let their little tirades get to you. As long as you are showing proper love and respect for your parents you don't have to feel guilty about not doing everything they expect you to do.

When you marry you become a part of your spouse's family, treat them with respect and someday you will come to love them. Never say anything detrimental about your in-laws to your spouse; he or she loves them no matter how weird they seem to you.

One of the nicest things you can do for your spouse is to be kind to his or her parents. If at all possible, become a real loving friend to them. Chances are you are going to need them in the days to come. Don't allow the green-eyed monster to get to you by making you jealous over any little attention that is shown to parents.

As you learn to leave you will find the cleaving part comes more easily. You and your spouse will be much happier as you look to each other for solutions to any problems that might occur. It is so nice to know that you have each other to cleave to during the pleasant times as well as the difficult times of life.

A Place for Friends

Something should be said about your friends and where they fit in your life after marriage. Life would be pretty dull without friends to enjoy, have fun with, and confide in. Friendships should be developed and nourished. After marriage you still need to cherish your friends but they will, and should, move down on your priority list

Sometimes a close friend that we have had for years may have an irritating personality to others. If your special friend irritates your spouse be considerate and do whatever is necessary to keep peace in your home. On the other hand there is no need to be jealous over a friendship if your spouse is treating you and the friendship as he or she should. You just need to come to some understanding about the time each of you give to friends and then make an effort to get along with the friends of the other.

The little Brownie song says, "Make new friends but keep the old, one is silver and the other is gold." Those words are so true, for friends are wonderful and you need to cherish the friends you have but remember your best friend should always be your spouse.

Fun and Relaxation

We are all different in what we like to do for fun and relaxation. Some enjoy spectator sports (football, basketball, baseball, hockey, etc.) while others like other sports activities such as hunting or fishing. Some like both and some don't like either. There are those who find reading a good book very relaxing and enjoyable. Whatever the activity, it must also move down on the priority list when you get married.

We have all heard of football widows - the cartoon shows a husband saying to his wife "do you have anything to tell me before the football season starts?" But to a wife who feels completely shut off from her husband during a particular ball season, it is no joke. Understanding and compromise are needed here. At times, you could watch a game together, but if you are not familiar with the game, don't say anything, it could be dangerous. Just be content in sitting close to him and knowing that you are doing this to stay connected. At other times allow your husband to watch his favorite game while you read a good book or watch an old movie.

A Neat Experience

One Saturday morning my husband and I were having breakfast at a fast food restaurant. We saw and talked to two very friendly ladies who were wearing their college team's football jersey. They enthusiastically told their expectations about the game that they would be attending that afternoon. Both ladies explained how their husbands did not like football so they left them at home. The wives seemed genuinely happy to be doing what they wanted to do and it seemed they left their husbands happy as well. This is what I am talking about; you can enjoy doing things that make you happy if you have taken time to be sure that your spouse is happy also. Seeing and hearing those ladies, who were great football fans, was such a neat experience for my husband and me.

Compromise Helps Keep Everyone Happy

I have also seen quite a few "hunting season widows." It seems that hunting can be quite a passion with some men. If you happen to be married to someone who loves (literally) to hunt, and this bothers you, please talk about it. You need to discuss how much he can hunt without making you unhappy. Don't wait until hunting season to tell him how you feel, the gleam in his eye will blind him to what you are trying to say. In reality, all these things should be discussed prior to marriage, but the eagerness to please each other often keeps this from happening.

Seriously, both of you should say how you feel and then come to some compromise that will make you both happy. When you compromise, your husband can leave home happy and then be eager to come home and get close to his understanding wife.

Gentlemen, here is a little tip for you. If your wife feels that you are close to her spiritually and emotionally when you are with her physically, she will be more willing to have you enjoy any sport you like. And ladies make your husband feel so good when he is with you spiritually and emotionally that he doesn't feel guilty when he watches a game or goes hunting, fishing, or any other type of recreation.

Some wives like to shop while others hate to shop. Some wives like to read while others hate to read. Whatever the activity a wife enjoys she should consider her husband and how he feels about it. Again, compromise. Husbands go shopping occasionally with your wife (without grumbling). At other times let her go alone and enjoy herself while you do something that you enjoy.

A Simple Solution May Work

When I was in graduate school I had to do an enormous amount of reading. My husband pastored a church at the time, so our time together was limited. My husband let me know that he wasn't pleased to find my nose always stuck in a book when he came home. Otherwise, he was always very supportive of my going on to graduate school. Knowing that it did not make him happy for me to always be reading, I would read until I heard his car turn into the driveway and then hurriedly put all my books away. I would then run to greet him at the door to let him know I was there for him, not just my physical presence but actually tuned in to his needs. I did this for several years and it worked beautifully.

Really Be There

Stop wrestling over what the other is doing or not doing, the goal is to make the other person feel so special that they will not mind you enjoying time out for what makes you happy. You do this by really being with the person when you are with them. You feel that emotional closeness that makes marriage so special. However, you can be in the same room with your spouse and not really be there.

The two of you may be sitting side by side on the sofa and you feel that you are enjoying quality time together. However, if you are sitting there engrossed in some television program you are not honestly spending time with each other. Your bodies just happen to be side by side and that is not what spending quality time with your spouse means. That is not to say that you can't enjoy a good show together but to always be glued to the television is not a way to give each other priority time. The television should occasionally be turned off and the two of you spend the evening talking about what is happening in your lives; if you haven't done this in a while you might find it hard to come up with something to talk about. Hang in there; you will finally learn to really talk with each other again.

Bonding

A couple needs the chance to bond to each other emotionally as well as physically. If parents, friends, children or anything else interferes with that bonding the couple cannot have the closeness their marriage deserves. Without that closeness the marriage will be less than what it should be and chances are it will not last. If the marriage survives it may become what is known as an empty shell marriage. An empty shell marriage is a marriage with no emotional closeness.

For various reasons many couples will stay in a marriage void of any emotional closeness for years. Over the years I have had many wives and a few husbands who have told me that after twenty or thirty years of marriage they wanted to call it quits. They would tell me that they did not want to spend the rest of their lives in a marriage without any closeness. The phrase I heard so often was "if this is all there is to marriage, I can't take it any more – I want out." By this time in the marriage they had become strangers living in the same household. They did not argue or fight – they just put up with each other.

The good news is when a couple really works at keeping each other first they will become closer as the years go by. Certainly there are times in any marriage when it is difficult to keep your spouse your number one priority. All through marriage - family relationships, parents, children, work, career and numerous other things will vie for your attention and emotional energy. But be careful that you never lose your focus in keeping your spouse and his or her needs first in your life. When you keep your spouse your focus both of you will reap the benefits of a marriage that will always remain close. Also when you make your spouse your first priority you are holding him or her close to you. By putting him or her first on your priority list you are making this person you have chosen to love forever feel very special and very much loved.

5

THE THRILL OF SEXUAL CLOSENESS

In every Marriage Seminar that I have conducted, this subject creates the most interest and vocal response. The reason for such interest is that most Christian couples want their sex life to be as fulfilling as God intended it to be. The good news is that it can be all that any couple ever imagined or hoped for. God designed sex for procreation and <u>recreation</u> so it is all right to enjoy sex with your spouse. Sex within marriage can give great pleasure and emotional fulfillment and it is completely moral, Hebrews 4:8 "The marriage bed is undefiled." The world is obsessed with sex and that is wrong, but that should not negate the fact that God intended for a husband and wife to enjoy a healthy sex life.

Not Scientific Research but It Sounds Great

Several years ago I read that *Redbook* magazine did a survey on the sex lives of 100,000 women. The results of the survey were quite a surprise because the religious women turned out to be the sexiest of all of the women who responded. I told about the *Redbook* survey in my Marriage and Family class and a young man quickly raised his hand and exclaimed, "Dr. Ray, I am going to start attending church." The young man's statement got quite a laugh. But, in reality, I think that Christian women as well as Christian men should enjoy, within marriage, the greatest sex life possible.

The ideal is for a couple to experience the joys of sex for the first time on their wedding night. This sounds wonderful, and many times it is, but don't be alarmed if, on your wedding night, it doesn't happen quite the way you thought it would. Many times the stress of a big wedding and all that goes with it put nerves on edge and that can create a problem in the sexual area. Don't worry and don't be disappointed, if things are not what you expected, just be patient. As you grow in your marriage you will also grow in your sexual relationship.

Adjustments Will Be Necessary

As in other areas of marriage, adjustments will have to be made in the sexual area. There are differences in sex drives. In general, the male has the greater sex drive, but I hasten to add, this is not always the case. If your husband has the greater sex drive naturally he will desire sex more often than you. You may be convinced that surely you married a sex maniac because all he seems to think about is sex. He, on the other hand, may think that something is wrong with you because you don't seem to be interested in sex very often. This can and will be worked out over time if you and your husband will talk openly and lovingly about meeting each other's sexual needs.

Different Strokes for Different Folks

Your sexual needs are different because the two of you are different. You differ in this area because you are male and female but also because your sexual needs and desires are part of your individual personality. Because each person is different, it is never safe to assume others feel as you do.

In other words, statements that all males are this way or all females are that way should never be made. I have learned from personal experience not to make any generalized statements about the sexual needs or desires of either male or female. To illustrate, let me share two different incidents with you.

I was teaching Marriage and the Family at a State University and I made the comment that men are usually sexually turned on by sight and women are turned on more by touch. Immediately one of the students, a young woman, raised her hand to say that she disagreed. She informed me that she, along with her mother and a few other ladies, went to a male strip show and the women who were there were very excited at seeing the male strippers. She went into great detail to tell me their response to what they saw. To say the least I was shocked, not only by her openness to share this with the whole class, but to think that she and her mother went to this place. This revelation did remind me that we have all been told what to expect of males and females sexually, but it safer not to assume that what is true for one is true for all. So, it is better not to say that all men are sexually turned on by sight and that all women are sexually turned on by touch. Everyone, males and females, are different in what excites them sexually.

An incident that occurred during a Marriage Seminar made me even more aware of how people differ in what excites them sexually. I told the ladies at the seminar that it would be nice if they would not go to bed wearing an old shirt and ball socks because that kind of attire would not be sexually appealing to their husbands. However, after the session a young lady informed me that her husband told her that he found her very sexy when she wore an old shirt and ball socks to bed. Once again I was made aware that what

49

might be a turn off for one person may sexually excite another. So, the moral of the story is for you, as a couple, to find out what excites and turns your spouse on sexually.

Aim to Please

I would like to encourage you ladies to pay more attention to what seems to please your husband than to do what the commercials and advertisements suggest you do in order to be sexy. Certain advertisements make you feel that if you would wear a certain fragrance or a particular undergarment you would be sexually attractive to your husband. Don't buy into their propaganda unless your husband says he would love to see you in something like what is being advertised. When you know your husband really wants you to wear a certain type of nightey – do your best to please him even if you feel "it isn't you." You will disappoint him if you tell him that you can't believe he would want you to wear something like that. Give him what he wants and make him happy – aim to please! Also, don't feel that you have to have a perfectly shaped body in order to wear something that he thinks would look sexy on you. Wear whatever it is he likes and don't worry about your not so perfect shape and chances are he won't notice the bumps and ridges in your body because he is will be so happy that you wanted to please him.

Cleanliness Makes It Easy to Get Close To You

Now for a word to the men about preparing their bodies to be sexually appealing to their wives. It is very important to most wives for their husbands to be clean-shaven or have a well-manicured beard before any attempt is made at lovemaking. It is just as important for the husband to be nice and clean as it is for the wife to be nice and clean. A good bath is always in order especially if you have been working hard all day. You want to come to your spouse with a clean body and fresh breath. We have all read the stories written to advice columnists about some husband that refuses to take a bath, or brush his teeth and he still expects his wife to be eager to have sex with him. It is hard for a wife to be turned on sexually when it is difficult for her to even get close to her husband because of the unpleasant odor she has to endure.

Another thing men, some women like the fragrance of a particular after-shave cologne, or to see you dressed a certain way. If your wife likes this kind of thing - don't be so macho, do your best to please her and you will reap the rewards. The best thing to do is to find out what will ignite her passion and then do your best to accommodate her.

A humorous illustration, provided by a wise young husband at a marriage retreat, expresses a little of what I have been trying to say in the area of practicing good hygiene. The young husband said that if he came home from work and heard a certain CD playing on the stereo, he would get very excited and go immediately to freshen up and take a shower. Why? Because he knew that the playing of that particular CD was his wife's signal that she was ready and waiting to enjoy sex with him. This story, though humorous, shows that this young husband was wise enough to know that a clean body is more sexually appealing. I don't want to belabor the point but I have heard too many stories of unclean bodies being a sexual turn-off so the importance of good hygiene cannot be overstated.

A Need for Discussion

Sex is something that you do need to discuss and believe it or not, it seems difficult for some couples to do.

There is no way that your spouse will know what you like or dislike in this area of your marriage unless you talk about what pleases you. You have to be honest with each other and say what turns you on sexually and what doesn't turn you on. Of course, please don't be cruel and say, "I can't stand it when you do that." Be kind and say, "I enjoy it when you do this (whatever is pleasurable to you) more than when you do that (whatever you find unpleasant). In one of my Marriage Seminars a wife related how she would gently guide her husband's hands to make him aware of what she found pleasurable.

If you want to try something different during your love making, be sure that your spouse feels okay with what you want to do. Sometimes one or the other will be more comfortable in experimenting during sex than the other, just remember that when you love someone you are considerate of his or her feelings. Talk about what you would enjoy doing and if both of you can't feel comfortable, then it is best not press the issue. Many good sexual unions have been ruined because one spouse would please himself or herself at the expense of the other.

No One Likes To Feel Used

A statement that I have heard from many wives is that they feel they are used sexually. They say that the only time they receive any attention from their husbands is when the husband wants sex. Husbands have responded to this accusation by saying that they don't know what she means when she says he doesn't give her any attention. This happens because wives are sometimes guilty of not saying what kind of attention they want or that they are expecting. Wives, you need to be very specific about what kind of attention you want so that your husbands will know what to do. It is a mistake on your part to think that your husband knows what you want when you say you need attention. Make sure you know what you need and then be very, very specific in telling your husband of your needs. For example, if a wife feels she would be getting the attention she wants if her husband would hug her during the day, or if he would kiss her several times every day, she should say that. Wives, whatever it is, tell your husbands so they won't have to play the guessing game. If you don't tell him, don't blame him if you feel used.

There are those husbands who say, "she's my wife and she should be ready to have sex with me anytime." If you feel your wife owes you sex just because she is your wife; you need to change your attitude. Sure, she is your wife and having sex is part of being married, but demanding sex is destructive to a healthy sex life. Husband, the good news is that if you give your wife the love and attention she needs, she will joyfully have, and enjoy, sex with you.

A Means of Expressing Love

There is a question that most counselors ask couples who come seeking help for their marriage. Regardless of the problem or problems they present, the counselor will usually ask the couple "How is your sex life?" The answer they give usually tells the counselor a lot about the marriage. It is not that sex is the most important thing in marriage, but it is important in determining the health of the marriage. When a couple is having trouble, it usually shows up in their sex life. Sex or withholding sex from a spouse is sometimes used as a method of control, alienation, or punishment. Sex is for expressing love and when it is withheld or is used as a weapon, it serves as a tool to destroy a marriage.

As a young minister's wife I was riding with a group of older ministers' wives and they decided to tell me a few things about married life. One piece of advice they gave me I knew then, as I know now, was not good advice. They told me if I ever wanted something, like a new dress, etc., a way to get my husband to purchase it was to offer to be good to him sexually in exchange for what I wanted. Even as a young inexperienced wife I knew that God did not intend that sex be used as a means of getting something I wanted. Sex is not a commodity that you bargain with. Ladies, your body already belongs to your husband just as his body belongs to you. When you love each other sex in marriage is an equal exchange.

In an earlier period in our history it was thought that ladies should not enjoy sex with their husbands. I was shocked to read that if a wife seemed to be enjoying the sex act her husband would become angry because he felt that she was an evil woman. This seems strange since we know that God made woman for the man **and** man for the woman. It is perfectly all right for the wife as well as the husband to enjoy and find pleasure in the sexual union.

You Are a Unique Couple

Remember you and your spouse are a unique couple. You are not like other couples so don't be guilty of comparing your sex life to others. In fact, you should not be sharing what goes on in this intimate part of your married life with anyone else. This is part of the beauty of sexual intimacy - it is private, just between you and your spouse. Also, be careful what you read, and what you watch on television and movies. Often times what these media portray is totally unrealistic and many times degrading and vulgar. You don't want these unholy images to invade the sanctity of your marriage bed.

You Don't Need the Filth

At the beginning of the counseling session all she could do was weep. When this young wife finally regained her composure she told me a very sad story. She related how she and her husband could not get excited sexually without watching a porno movie. She said it all began when they started watching the porno channels on TV and then they started going to "peep shows". The more they watched the more perverted the sex had to be in order to excite them sexually. After she told me this story she wept and said, "I feel so dirty." Her story was particularly tragic to me, because it did not have to be. As a couple you have each other to enjoy and you don't need anything to stimulate your sexual appetite but your love for each other. You can find many exciting and thrilling ways to enjoy sex together and not feel guilty.

Use Your Imagination

It has been said that our most important sex organ is our mind. It is in our mind that we develop a healthy or an unhealthy attitude toward sex. I often suggest to wives that they use their God given imagination to think of how wonderful it is to have sex with their husbands. Prepare your mind as well as your heart, to be ready for him when he needs you sexually. If you want to see a happy husband let him know that you have been imagining what sex would be like when you came together. We are told that a man has to be satisfied with the sexual area before he can be satisfied with the whole marriage. And wives, you are the key to his satisfaction. The bottom line is to talk, don't bottle up your feelings, if you do, you will not experience the closeness that sexual intimacy brings.

Believe it or not, children, work, career or a hundred other things can hinder your sex life. It is true that there are times in most marriages where the demands of raising a family and becoming established in a career make it difficult to have time for each other. You feel you simply cannot find the time or the energy, but you must make time for sex. Sex can bring comfort, assurance, and encouragement. In fact, the sex act releases certain chemicals in your body that can help relieve stress, and calm your nerves. I made the statement in one seminar that if a wife was nervous sometimes it would help bring relief if she had sex with her husband. At that point, I had many husbands asking their wives if they didn't feel nervous. They were very much concerned for their wives and they wanted them to know that they were available to help with their nervous condition. However, it is no joke that sex is good for your overall health and to stay healthy you need to keep having sex as long as you can.

What about This Romance Thing?

Romance means different things to different people. Some wives enjoy having their husbands give them flowers or candy; to them this is romance. For others romance is a candlelight dinner or sitting in front of a roaring fire holding or being held close by the one they love. Believe it or not, romance to some is when they are riding a Honda with their arms wrapped tightly around their beloved. Romance really happens when we feel especially close and loving toward our soul mate regardless of where we are or what we are doing. You feel connected to each other in an un-earthy sort of way.

Some would have us to believe that to have romance in our marriage we have to make love by candlelight. Making love by candlelight can be romantic, but candlelight is not for everybody. A wife might buy into this candlelight thing and have candles lighted throughout the bedroom only to have her husband make some thoughtless remark about not being able to see. This may make the wife feel that her husband is not romantic. The husband, on the other hand, might feel very romantic when they snuggle together on the couch in a brightly-lighted room.

As with everything we have mentioned, talk about what you think is romantic and once you understand what the other wants, try your best to please him or her. You can take turns doing what the other considers romantic. Have the romantic candlelight occasionally; knowing that you are pleasing your spouse, and then your spouse will do whatever it is that gives you a feeling of romance. That is love and accommodation.

When both of you are doing what you can to please each other, you develop a love cycle. Each spouse tries to outdo the other in finding ways to show their love. Isn't that wonderful? A love cycle brings the closeness that each spouse really needs and wants. When this happens it is easy to enjoy the thrill of sexual closeness.

6

FUMING, FUSSING, AND FIGHTING

Sounds like a hillbilly ballad doesn't it? Sooner or later, in most marriages, a little bit of fuming, fussing, and fighting goes on. In professional marriage and family circles, they call it conflict, and they agree that conflict can be good for a marriage.

In reality, it is the way you handle conflict that makes the difference; it can draw you closer or drive you apart.

A Shocking Discovery

As a young bride I entered marriage expecting (unrealistically) that my husband and I would agree on everything, after all, we loved each other and we were Christians. It took about two weeks to discover that there were a lot of things about which we disagreed. To be honest I was shocked and hurt that we would get so upset with each other. We had not been taught that conflict in a marriage is inevitable and neither had we been taught how to deal with conflict.

I just didn't think that Christian couples should have arguments or become so angry that hurtful things would be said in the middle of a disagreement. We did not know how to deal with our frustrations and the anger we felt. We would either let our anger explode in a very unproductive way or we would fume in silence as we nursed our grievances.

It took several years for us to understand that if our marriage was going to be what it should be we had to learn to "fight fair." With growth, education, and God's help we finally understood that we were two different individuals who would not always agree on everything and that need not be a problem.

Conflict Really Can Be Positive

You and your spouse should try to accept conflict as something that can be positive to your relationship. With a more positive attitude toward conflict you will find it easier to handle misunderstandings. When misunderstandings happen, you will not be blown out of the water and you will also be more likely to come up with a way of resolving the problem. Conflict dealt with in this way can be good for the marriage. The key words here are "resolve" and "positive." This is where the work comes in. Learning to deal with the everyday frustrations without losing your cool is quite an accomplishment and one that doesn't come easy for most individuals. For conflict to be a good thing and lead to a closer relationship, you, as a couple need to deal with each problem as it happens.

Fuming

In most instances, it is easier to fume over something that you feel has not gone your way in the relationship. You can fume by not talking to your spouse; this is called the "silent treatment." Somehow there is something about the silent treatment that makes you feel righteous. You feel as long as you are not arguing, throwing insults, and other unrighteous things, you are in the clear. However, fuming about something that was said or done to you is a sneaky way of getting back at your spouse.

You are not doing yourself any favor either by fuming instead of admitting your anger. Not dealing with your anger can lead to backaches, headaches, and all kinds of physical and emotional problems. Maybe you think that if you just keep quiet things will get better. Chances are the underlying cause of your conflict will not go away until you deal with it.

According to the dictionary when you are fuming you are in a state of excited irritation or anger. Whether you realize it or not you are giving off some mighty bad fumes by your attitude even if you are not saying anything. Your silence, your facial expression, and your posture can be difficult for your spouse to deal with. To put it plainly, fuming is not fair fighting.

When you are fuming you are not giving your spouse the benefit of responding to your anger. It is frustrating to try to talk with someone who will not answer, look the other way or will walk out of the room. When this happens over and over, your spouse will probably say "what is the use of trying to talk to you, I give up." That is when the distance between the two of you begins and you lose the closeness you once shared. Fuming is not good for a relationship because you are silently destroying your marriage.

Fussing

Fussing or expressing your anger is not good for your relationship because you usually say things to hurt the other person. When you are fussing, not fuming, it is true that you are expressing your anger but expressing anger in order to win over your spouse can be harmful to a relationship.

The right way to express anger is to admit that you are angry and what you are angry about to the person with whom you are angry. Did you follow me? Just say to your spouse, "I am angry about this," whatever it is you are angry about. You may use any of these words; angry, upset, or mad. Just don't say "you made me angry, upset or mad." Using "you" at this point will pour fuel on the fire and the conflict will not get resolved in a positive way. After all, no other person can make you angry or mad. This is something you allow yourself to become because someone has said or done something that you did not like.

When you are in a conflict or battle it is better to state only what you are feeling and ask for help in dealing with that feeling. For instance, you might say something like, "I am upset (angry) over our finances and I need your help in dealing with it, instead of "You have made a mess of our finances, you just don't know how to handle money." When you use the latter statement the other person feels attacked and he or she immediately plans a counter attack.

Fighting –Verbal Abuse

Counter attacks can get pretty messy. No weapon is considered too dirty to use in order to win the fight. A powerful weapon often used is to drag up everything that has gone wrong in the past, the old arguments that were never settled or better still the old hurts that have not healed. Sometimes angry feelings toward in-laws or relatives are expressed to try to hurt the other person. Statements such as "you are just like your mother, she could not handle money either." "That is why your family never had anything." Those words call for your spouse to use even more destructive weapons to hurt you. The fight then escalates and can lead to name calling or what

61

is known as "hitting below the belt." Please steer clear of statements like, "You are (stupid, dumb, crazy, etc.) for feeling the way you do." When you make a statement like that you are making a verbal attack on the person you are supposed to love and respect.

When the conflict reaches this stage things are said or done that can cause major damage to the relationship.

Fighting – Physical Abuse

It is at this stage of fighting when both husband and wife are so angry that it is very easy for physical abuse to occur. This is so sad because usually the abusive person could not have imagined that he or she would have ever hit or pushed his or her spouse. Physical abuse is humiliating, it is dangerous, and it is definitely destructive to a marriage. So many times I have heard the statement, "I never thought I would be guilty of physically abusing my wife." Yet, physical abuse happens when a husband or wife allows anger to completely control him or her.

So often we think abuse only happens when there is alcohol involved. Think again. When people, who would never think of taking a drink of alcohol, get into a blind rage they are capable of anything. In the heat of anger, sweet, loving and kind people have been known to do things they thought themselves incapable of doing.

I was visiting with a very close friend and she very sadly related to me how she became so angry with her husband that she threw a pie at him. She went on to say how she never thought she could be guilty of ever doing anything that was so contrary to her personality. It was difficult for me to believe also. She was such a sweet and kind individual. So, what I am saying is this – don't let your anger control you, you control your anger.

Understand Your Anger

I would suggest that when you are angry that you take time to make yourself sit down and feel that anger. After you have allowed yourself to feel your anger, then determine what you are really angry about. It is surprising how often we allow ourselves to get upset or angry and blow our stacks when, in reality, we don't know the real cause of our anger. When we determine the real cause of our anger we can then deal with it in a sensible way. Just remember, that anger that is expressed in order to hurt the other person is very destructive to a close relationship.

When you are trying to diffuse an angry situation by acknowledging your anger use only "I" statements and say what you are feeling in a way that doesn't sound like you are accusing your spouse of causing whatever it is that you are upset about. Handling conflict in a positive way means taking responsibility for your own feelings and being specific about how you feel about the problem.

Don't Deny His or Her Right to be Angry

Another thing to remember when there is conflict between you and your spouse is to learn to validate each other's feelings. When your spouse is angry, don't negate his or her feeling by saying that he or she should not be angry. If a person feels angry, he or she is angry, and denying the person's feelings does not make those feelings go away.

Husbands, if your wife is angry please don't try to tell her that she is not angry or should not have those angry feelings. If she says she is angry - she feels angry. Validate her feelings by giving her a sympathetic hug and saying, "I know that you are feeling very angry right now, is there anything I can do?" She might tell you to get out of her

63

sight, if she does, oblige her. Wait until she calms down and then try to discuss the situation.

And wives, your husbands need to have their feelings validated as well. If you can say it and be honest, tell him that he has a right to be angry. Wait a while before trying to talk about the problem. There needs to be a cooling off period so that both you and your husband can get control of your feelings. But you do need to allow each other the privilege to feel anger over a situation and work at trying to make your home a safe place for any anger to be acknowledged without fear of causing an unfair fight.

Conflict in marriage can become a stepping-stone to greater intimacy or it can become a stumbling block to a close relationship. Learn to resolve conflict creatively by finding ways that will help to diffuse an angry and tense situation. Some couples use humor, but a word of caution is needed here – you need to be very careful how you use humor. Humor can pour fuel on the fire if your spouse feels that he or she is the target and that you are being sarcastic. If you use humor, direct it at yourself or at the situation, not at your spouse. Not too many people are capable of using humor to resolve conflict in a positive way – it usually leads to more trouble, so be careful!

As a couple you might agree on a phrase or word to be used by either when a situation seems to be getting out of hand. Think creatively – you are trying to build your relationship, not tear it down. Remember it is all in the way conflict is handled. Learn to handle it wisely and as the years go by you will grow closer and the conflicts between you will become fewer in number. However, conflict will never go away completely because you are two different people and you will never see eye to eye on everything but you can still remain cheek to cheek.

7

COMMUNICATION

It almost goes without saying that communication is a big problem in marriage. Most experts in the field of marriage will tell you that an effective communication system is essential to a happy marriage. The problem seems to be that couples do not really understand how to communicate in a way that is satisfying to both of them.

Sure – We Talk

In a counseling session, when a couple is asked whether or not they communicate, the male usually says yes, that he and his wife talk all the time. What he means is they talk about surface things. Such things as "who is going to pick up the children at Daycare," or "did we get any mail today?' What the husband fails to realize is that these are just conversations about everyday things that do not require any investment of himself. On the other hand, the wife usually replies that they "never" communicate. What she means is they talk but she doesn't feel like the talking they do is on any kind of personal level. She wants to have more personal communication. As a result, she feels something is missing from the marriage and she is right. Without good communication it is hard to truly know your spouse.

An effective communication system requires that the conversations between husband and wife need to, at times, get beyond the surface level. The start of good communication is to put some of who you are and what you are feeling into the conversation. However, intimate communication, communication that brings you closer to each other, happens when each of you share your feelings openly and honestly with each other. In order to communicate on this level both husband and wife have to feel safe enough in the relationship to share their true feelings. Neither spouse will feel free to reveal anything personal if there is a fear of being criticized or made fun of. A close and loving relationship creates an environment where each spouse feels safe in stating his or her true feelings in love.

Know What You Want To Say

To really get across to your spouse what it is that you want them to know you must first think it through in your own mind. Get your thoughts in order by asking yourself what it is that you want to convey to your spouse. You do this by filtering out everything that does not pertain to what you are trying to say. Focus only on what it is that you want him or her to hear and understand. Be sure you have your spouse's attention before you begin the conversation by asking that he or she please put aside everything else and listen. Of course, you make this request in a non-threatening way.

As you begin the conversation try to be as specific as possible in saying what you are thinking or feeling. That is why it is so important for you to know what you are thinking or feeling about any situation before you try to explain it to someone else. Sometimes we are so confused over something that when we try to convey it to our spouse it is hard for him or her to really understand. It is necessary that you be very specific in saying what it is that you want your spouse to know.

Many times in counseling couples I ask the wife what she really wants or expects from her husband. On occasion the wife would answer, "I just want him to show me more love." The husband would say, "I love her and I tell her I love her." She would interrupt and say, "but that is not enough." The husband would look exasperated and ask, "What can I do?" It is all a matter of being specific. As the couple's counselor I would ask the wife, "What exactly do you want him to do to show you more love?" Do you want him to hug you more, kiss you more, just what do you want? We would finally get down to the nitty gritty – the wife wants you to hug her four times a day and kiss her when you leave, when you come home, and before you go to sleep. Sometimes we have a tendency to think that our spouse should know what we want without our having to be so specific. No Way! Neither husbands or wives have the gift of mind reading. Make sure you know what you want and make sure he or she understands what you want.

A Listening Ear with a Mind to Hear

Another problem in communication is not really listening to what the other person is saying. Listening is a part of good communication. Pay attention, be an active listener – make eye contact, nod your head, in some way let your spouse know that you are listening. Sometimes it helps to validate what you thought you heard. You do this by saying something like, "This is what I heard you say," then repeat what you heard." When you do this it gives the speaker a chance to say, "Yes, that is what I said, or no, that is not what I said." It is not necessary to do this every time but sometimes it helps makes things clearer to the speaker and the hearer.

Honesty with Love

To have clear communication you have to be honest with each other and at the same time be supportive. When you are trying to get something across to your spouse use love and not anger. He or she will come closer to understanding and doing something about what you are asking for if you speak in love. When you speak in love you don't criticize and do remember there is no such thing as friendly criticism. We all have a tendency to focus on what is not done or not done right. Focus on the positive not the negative.

Just Take Care of It

The combination of what the male is biologically and how he was reared has prepared him to think logically when faced with problems. When faced with a difficult situation or problem, the female is guided more by her feelings. When the female just wants to express what she is feeling concerning a situation, the male takes on the instrumental role and says, "Do something about it, take care of it." He is for solving the problem while she just wants to talk about it.

For instance, let's just say she gets upset at work and when she comes home she unloads on her husband. She says, "I can hardly stand to go to work anymore, my boss is so hard to get along with and I can't seem to please him no matter what I do." Now, keep in mind, she just wants to "express" her feelings, at the same time, hoping that her husband will sympathize and understand her feelings. He, being the male that he is, answers, "You just need to quit that job and find another one where the boss will be nicer to you." This upsets his wife because she just wanted him to listen and understand. She would never think of quitting her job and she tells him so. On the other hand, he gets upset because he feels that he wasted his breath, she never does what he suggests. She was thinking like a female and he was thinking like a male.

What happened was a typical male and female reaction to a problem. Females want to talk about their problem and males want to fix the problem. What would have helped in this particular scenario? When the wife made the statement that she could hardly stand to go to work because of her boss, the husband could have avoided a little frustration by saying, "I understand that you are upset, is there anything I can do? She could answer, "I don't think so, just let me talk about it." By making such a simple statement he has just shown her that he heard her and he cares about what she is feeling. By being honest in her answer she was letting him know that all she wanted him to do was to listen while she unloaded all of her frustrations.

Believe it or not that is all she wanted. Males are prone to think, "why talk about it if you don't want to do something about it." Husbands, it would be great for you if you could learn, "don't try to fix, just try to listen." When you try to fix her problem she doesn't feel the caring and concern that she wants to feel. It is the same thing we have talked about – it is a feeling of closeness that she feels when you try to understand her feelings of frustration.

It Is My Turn

Have you ever tried to have a conversation with someone who would not let you talk? The other person would · not stop long enough to let you say a word in response to what he or she said. This can be very frustrating. In a marriage each spouse should have a chance to speak when something is being discussed. In an enjoyable and fruitful conversation a person is given a chance to talk and the other person is then given the chance to respond. If you do not give your spouse a chance to respond you are robbing him or her of the chance to express what he or she is feeling. When someone is constantly denied the opportunity to say what he or she is feeling, resentment starts to build. After a while, the resentment will lead to complete withdrawal. An attitude of "What's the use?" develops. This attitude and withdrawal is a sure way to grow apart rather than growing closer. You cannot know another person if you do not allow him or her to express his or her feelings concerning whatever is being discussed.

In counseling, I have often used an egg timer to allow each spouse his or her turn in speaking about a particular issue. When one is speaking, the other is not allowed to say a word until his or her time to speak. I am sure you would not be surprised to hear that often times it is very difficult for the person not speaking to keep quiet until the other is finished. We all have a tendency to cut the other person off in order to say what we think or feel, but go back to what you were taught as a child – Take Turns. Let the other person finish and then respond.

Completed Sentences

There is something that we, as wives, have a tendency to do. We get into the habit of finishing our husbands' sentences. On one occasion when I was visiting my mother she was visited by a couple that had been married several years. As we sat there I cannot count the times when the husband would start to tell something and she would finish. I took notice that he would just stop talking and let her finish – with a sigh of resignation. In other words he was used to this happening but he still did not find it easy to take. Ladies, it might surprise you to know that your husband can actually finish his own sentences.

The tendency to finish my husband's sentences or feeling that I have to explain what he is saying is something that I have to continue to work on. I am sorry to say that when we were much younger and just beginning in the ministry I made quite a few mistakes along this line. We would visit our church members and on occasion when my husband would be asked a biblical question I would feel he needed my help so I would jump in to rescue him. Being young I did not realize how that must have made him feel or how it looked to the members we were visiting. When I learned that doing this was not making him feel good about himself, I knew I had to control my behavior and my tongue. When I allowed my husband to answer without my interference, he did a terrific job. As a result, he felt better about himself, better about me, and I even felt better knowing that I had not interfered.

Another thing that we must be cautious about is correcting each other over minute details. And again ladies, I am sorry to say that most of the time we are the guilty ones. The husband might say we had to travel thirty miles to such and such place and the wife says, "Oh no, it was twenty-nine and one-half miles." What difference does it really make? I must confess this happened to me the other night over some small detail that I felt it was my duty to correct. When we do this we interrupt the other person's train of thought and it often creates awkwardness in the conversation. It also, if I may say so, makes the person

71

who is talking feel dumb! We should do our best to keep the tongue under control.

Nonverbal Communication

Would you believe that some authorities suggest that as much as sixty-five (65%) of all face-to-face communication is nonverbal? A lot of our communication is done through our body language. We communicate to others by the way we sit, stand, look, dress, grunt, sigh, the way we use our hands and even by the way we smell.

When we are saying one thing and our nonverbal behavior is communicating something else, the nonverbal behavior carries more weight. For instance, a husband notices that his wife seems very cool toward him and he asks her what is wrong. She straightens her back, perhaps tightens her lip and replies, "Nothing." She is saying nothing is wrong but her nonverbal behavior is saying otherwise. The "wise" husband knows something is wrong and he will gently try to find out what it is and then take the necessary steps to make it right.

What Does It Matter?

I have a problem with wives who do everything they can to look nice before they marry and then once married, they let themselves go. When a wife doesn't even bother to comb her hair when she gets up in the morning, she is saying to her husband, "you are not worth the effort any more." A wife might think that her husband doesn't even notice her so she develops the attitude that it doesn't really matter how she looks. Regardless of what a wife might think she should always try to look her best for her husband. I am not talking about getting up early to completely fix your face or as my husband says, "go through complete urban renewal, but please don't greet him looking like the last rose of summer. He deserves more than that – just think, he'll take the vision of you with him all day. Make it a good one. It really does matter!

That Old Robe

Forgive me, but there are women who have worn the same robe or housecoat for years and their husbands would probably love to see the robe thrown away or burned. Think of it this way. Would you want your best girlfriend to see you in that robe? Doesn't your husband mean more to you than your best girlfriend? Yes, a worn out robe is communicating to your husband that you feel it is only important to fix up for others – not him. Shame, shame, go out and buy a new robe, spritz on some cologne and greet that husband with a kiss. He will love you for it!

Why Be Burly?

Now, for you husbands. You need to take notice of how you greet your wife in the morning. Don't come to the table with your hair all tousled and your shirt off because if you do, you are nonverbally communicating to your wife that you don't care how you look to her. Do whatever is necessary to make her know that you are just as concerned over how you appear to her as you were before she married you. She will love you for it!

Everyday Things Matter

A word to both husbands and wives. Be sure to practice good hygiene. You not only need to look nice but you need to smell nice. Of course you know you do this by brushing your teeth, bathing regularly, and putting on clean clothes. It is easier to get close to someone who looks and smells nice. These are all ways in which couples can communicate nonverbally their love and respect for each other.

Look and Really See

Another way of learning to communicate is to practice noticing everything about your spouse. When you look at your spouse really see him or her. Notice what he or she has on, his or her countenance – everything! When you do this you are becoming aware and you are showing that you really care enough to take a good look.

In my marriage seminars I do a little fun exercise by asking the husbands to close their eyes and then I ask how many can describe the type of jewelry that their wives are wearing, the color of shoes, etc. It is amazing how many husbands do not have any idea the jewelry, shoes or any other article of clothing their wives are wearing. Of course I repeat the exercise asking wives to describe their husbands clothing, but it doesn't work as well. The wives laugh and say, "We should know, we are the ones who told our husbands what to wear tonight." Be that as it may, the exercise does make a point; many times we don't take time to really see the other person.

You have probably heard the story of the wife who came out of her bedroom without any clothes on and announced to her husband she was going to the mall. He was so engrossed in watching a game on TV that he waved his hand and replied, "Sure, honey, go ahead and have a good time." Wow! She was really trying to make a point. I think she made it! Take time to look and really see your spouse, not only what he or she is wearing (or not wearing) but also the facial expression, posture and anything else that might give you a clue as to what he or she might be feeling.

You Are Still Special

Please continue to practice good ole fashion manners! Use those kind words, "please," and "thank you." Somehow we think we only use these words with those outside our home or they are words to be taught to our children, but they are words that we should use frequently in communicating with our spouse. I often use the illustration of how when a young woman walks in front of her fiancé and happens to stumble over his feet they will both politely say, "excuse me." However, the scene often changes after marriage – she walks in front of her husband, stumbles over his feet, and exclaims, "Get your big feet out of the way." He replies, "hey, watch where you are going." Being polite and courteous to each other should never change; in fact, it should increase with each year of marriage.

Sometimes husbands and wives get into a vicious cycle of hurting each other with words and disrespectful behavior. However, it is so much better for a marriage if a couple can get into a blessed cycle of trying to outdo one another in showing genuine kindness and old fashioned courtesy. Husbands, treat your wife like a queen and she will respect you as her king. I know we are living in a liberated society and some women do not like to have doors opened for them, however, it is your job to find out the courtesies your wife would like shown to her. And dear wife, if your husband opens a door for you, pulls your chair out for you, or shows you kindness in any way, please don't forget to say a pleasant "thank you." Please do not be guilty of saying, "What did you do that for?" or "You are just doing that because you were told it was the nice thing to do." Be the gracious lady as he is the courteous gentleman. Life becomes so much more genteel with this kind of behavior. I get a warm feeling inside just writing about these genuine expressions of kindness – I can almost smell the fragrance of roses!

In concluding this chapter on communication, there is just this reminder – Communication is a lot more than just saying words!

8

CHRISTIAN COMMITMENT
OR CONTROVERSY

Many studies have shown that when couples have some kind of religious commitment the likelihood of their marriage lasting is greater than it is for those couples who do not profess any faith or religion. These studies should be an encouragement to you and your spouse if you have committed your lives to God. However if you have not included God in your marriage, you are now aware that this commitment will help you personally, and also be a source of strength in your marriage. It is wonderful to be able to ask for God's help in your marriage and it is also wonderful to belong to a community of faith that will stand with you when you are struggling with marital difficulties.

The Need for God's Help

It is certainly true that we all need God's help in overcoming the difficulties that we will encounter in this wonderful adventure of marriage. I personally know that without God's love and guidance in our marriage some problems would have been more difficult, if not impossible, to overcome. In fact, just today someone asked my husband and me if we had ever had any problems in our marriage. Without hesitation we both answered, "Yes, we had major problems when we were first married and if it had not been for our faith and trust in God, we would not have made it." This young lady went on to say that we appear to be so happy and genuinely in love now that she could not believe that we had ever had any problems. I told her that we not only "appear" to be in love, we "Are" in love but, we have had, problems in our marriage. So you see, with God's help you can overcome your difficulties and have a greater marriage than ever, a marriage that will be an encouragement to others.

If you are not married you might think that your Christian faith is not a big issue and certainly not one that would cause a problem between you and your future spouse. However, as a counselor, I can tell you that Christian faith and commitment often become more significant to an individual after marriage. As stated earlier, a person's personal commitment to his or her faith can be a source of strength in the marriage, but at this point I want to approach the subject of commitment from a different perspective. The issue I want to discuss happens when a husband or wife becomes overly involved in church related activities to the detriment of their marriage.

Church Involvement Issues

It would be great if engaged couples discussed their Christian commitment in great detail before marriage. However, the important thing to most couples, at this point in the relationship, is that they are of the same religious faith. Being of the same faith is important but there are church involvement issues that should also be discussed. Problems could be avoided if time was spent talking about their feelings regarding the giving of their time, talent, and money. It would also be helpful if each one would be open, honest and specific about his or her personal commitment to God and to the church.

A Distraught Wife

Tina sat before me distraught over the fact that her husband was neglecting her because he was always working at their church. Harry was not a minister but he had made a personal commitment to help at the church as much as possible. Tina felt that he was overly committed to the church and not committed enough to her and their marriage. She was angry because Harry spent so many evenings working at the church and if that wasn't enough he also spent each church service helping with the sound system, leaving her to sit alone. Tina said that she had cried and told Harry that what he was doing was not right and that God did not require him to spend so much time at the church. Harry did not listen to her pleas to spend more time at home and with her. Now here she is with tears in her eyes telling me that she feels the church is Harry's mistress and she is competing with the church for his attention. They were wrestling over church involvement issues and as a result the marriage was in trouble.

An Irate Husband

On another occasion a young husband told me that he could not continue to put up with his wife spending so much time at the church involved in music ministry. In her presence he told me how their marriage, home, and children were being neglected. She too, like the young man in the example above, felt that because of her musical talent that it was her duty to be that involved. In this case, a husband and children were being neglected because a wife and mother failed to realize that after a personal relationship with God that husband, home, and family should come before anything else.

Setting Priorities

Situations like the two mentioned above happen because we do not have our priorities right. We need to prioritize our relationships by putting them in the proper order. Our personal relationship with God is first, our relationship with our spouse second, our relationship with our children next, and then our relationship and involvement with our church. The problem occurs when the relationship with God and the relationship with the church get confused. There is a difference. Involvement in church activities should not supercede our involvement with our spouse and family. God expects all of us to obey His Word by loving and respecting our spouse, and to understand that our children are the heritage of the Lord. When His Word is obeyed we can expect to have a close and loving relationship with our spouse, family and the church.

Another Tragic Story

Just a few days ago I was told the tragic story of a wife and mother who, when she received Christ as her Savior, became so involved in church she neglected her husband and family. Her husband told a co-worker how his wife would stay at the church all the time while unwashed dishes would be stacked on the counter, dirty clothes piled in the floor and beds left unmade. As a result, the couple was getting a divorce. This is tragic and it happens all too often.

First Things First

Several years ago I was one of several speakers at a large Women's Convention. A young enthusiastic speaker, when it came her turn to speak, walked to the pulpit and made this announcement to that great crowd of ladies, "If your commode at home ain't clean you don't have any right to be here rejoicing; go home and clean your commode first and then you can rejoice." What was she saying? She was telling that group of ladies to put first things first. When things are kept in their proper order there will be a lot less wrestling over church related issues.

Get It Together

As a couple you need to pray about and discuss how involved each of you should be in church ministries and activities. The church does need those who are willing to give of their time and talent but most pastors would not want couples having difficulties over one spouse or the other being overly involved. Good healthy churches need good healthy families. When you, as a couple, agree over this issue your family and church will both benefit.

Personal Expressions of Faith

You might be a person who is very verbal and vocal about your personal relationship with God and that is to be commended. However, it would be good to remember that your spouse may be very different from you in the way he or she expresses his or her faith. The expectation that your spouse will also be vocal about his or her personal relationship with God may lead to disappointment. Accept that your spouse is different from you and please refrain from trying to make him or her feel guilty over not being as expressive as you are. Trying to make a person feel guilty only makes matters worse, it doesn't change anything.

A nice lady approached me at a Women's Retreat and informed me that she had not seen her husband reading his

Bible or praying like he should. She went on to ask me what she should do about his lack of commitment. I immediately thought, "Lady, who made you a spiritual detective?" I could just see her peeking around the corner to see if she could catch her husband reading his Bible or praying. Of course, we should be concerned about our spouse's spiritual condition, but we certainly don't make it any better by spying on him or her. When we sense that our spouse has a spiritual need we should talk to the Lord about it. Praying about his or her spiritual need will help us to keep the right attitude and a sweet spirit. We should never try to act super spiritual when we are in the presence of our spouse thinking it will make him or her want to measure up. This kind of attitude is not appreciated and it will do more harm than good. People who try to be so super spiritual make others want to gag.

Several years ago I was counseling a couple who had major marital problems. It was difficult for me to counsel this couple because the husband always brought his Bible to the counseling sessions. All during the session the husband would thump the Bible with his hand as he quoted scripture to me and to his wife. Of course the scriptures were carefully chosen in order to put a guilt trip on his wife and to try to impress me with his great spirituality. Neither his wife nor I could appreciate his apparent hypocrisy being displayed as super spirituality. To use a bit of common vernacular, "Come off of it," your spouse (and others) knows if you are real or plastic. The best and most important thing you can do for your spouse is to make it a priority to pray for his or her walk with the Lord.

The Spiritual Leader

We honor God's Word by recognizing that He has established the man as the spiritual leader in the home.

Sometimes a husband/father may be too timid to read or pray openly in front of his wife and children. When this happens a wife should not despair but lovingly encourage her husband without preaching to him about his rightful duties. A wife can show she respects him as the head of their household and as time passes it is possible that he will become more secure in fulfilling his role as the spiritual leader. This is a matter that a wife/mother should also take to the Lord in prayer.

It is a beautiful thing when a couple feels comfortable enough to pray together during their engagement or at the beginning of their marriage. At the beginning of our marriage my husband was a little shy about praying together but after a while we felt comfortable enough to join hands and hearts in prayer. We also have our personal quiet time and devotions. When I hear him praying in the other room it brings tears to my eyes for I know he prays for me just as I pray for him.

An Unsaved Spouse

Maybe some of you who are reading this book have an unsaved spouse. I know that makes your walk with the Lord more difficult but please know that prayer and a sweet, kind, disposition on your part, can work wonders in winning your spouse to the Lord.

1 Peter 3:1-2
Wives, in the same way be submissive to your husbands so that, if any of them do not believe the word, they may be won over without words by the behavior of their wives, 2 when they see the purity and reverence of your lives.

We have often told our parishioners, who had unsaved companions, not to preach, or try to cajole but with a meek and quiet spirit show them an extra amount of agape

83

(unconditional) love. This kind of love mixed with prayer will do wonders!

In concluding this chapter I want to emphasize that with time and sincere effort, on the part of both spouses, problems in Christian faith and commitment can be worked out beautifully. We need to feel secure enough in our marriage to discuss openly and honestly our relationship with God and our spiritual needs and goals. When we do this we are drawn closer together and we really do become soul mates.

9

MONEY DOES MATTER

Couples do not usually talk about money, they fight about money. In fact they tell us that eighty percent of couples seeking divorce state that the focus of their disagreements is money. One of the reasons that couples fight about money is that husbands and wives often have different value systems.

Family Background

We have already established that we are a product of how we were reared and needless to say, it is true also in how we feel about money. A wife might have grown up in a family where the lack of money was not a problem and as a result she feels free to spend whatever money is available. On the other hand her husband might have been reared in a family where money was tight and he was taught to spend money very cautiously. These two get married and their value systems collide. She wants to spend and he wants to save – the wrestling match begins.

To help in money matters you and your spouse need to talk about your feelings regarding money and what money means to each of you. When you understand each other's feelings regarding money you can make better choices about how you spend or what you will put aside in savings.

Also, you need to realize that for most couples marriage is a future reward system. You should not expect to have, at the beginning of your marriage, all of the material things that your parents have. Remember it took years for your parents to accumulate all that they have. Some couples want to have everything at once; they are not willing to wait until they are more comfortable financially. When they do try to buy all the nice things, they sometimes get themselves in a financial strain which, in turn, puts a strain on their marriage.

Be Careful How You Charge

Years ago I was listening to the radio while driving in a large city and the radio announcer said, "Ladies, it is a beautiful day in the city, a day to go out and charge, charge, charge." I could envision ladies hurriedly getting dressed, grabbing their charge cards and hitting the department stores. I hasten to add that it is not just the ladies who get caught in the charge net, men can also get caught. It can happen to anybody, we must all be careful about using those charge cards.

It is so easy to charge, charge, charge, but using a credit card to buy things that you could wait about getting until you have the money, spells disaster for your bank account and your marriage. It almost goes without saying that when you charge, most of the time you end up paying a double price for whatever you buy – the interest rate on credit cards is extremely high. If you do use a credit card you need to pay the entire balance each month to avoid paying the high interest. It would be much better if you just wait until you have the money to buy what you think you need. Often times if you wait, you will find out that you really did not need that particular item after all. When I see something that think I need, I ask myself, "Do I really need this or will I really use this?" Most of the time asking and answering these two questions keeps me from spending money needlessly.

Very Wise Advice

When my husband, Jesse, and I were very young he was called to pastor a small church in a little town in South Georgia. This was our first pastorate and there were a lot of things we did not know about shepherding a spiritual flock. However, we were blessed with some very wise, elderly parishioners who taught us so many things. One elderly deacon was very respectful to the leadership of the pastor but he became a wonderful mentor to Jesse. At the same time, the deacon's wife and several other godly ladies became my mentors. They taught me how to cook old fashioned cakes and pies and they taught me how to sew clothes for our children. But the one thing that I remember so vividly is the advice the deacon's wife gave me regarding money. She said to me, "What you need to do is to make you a "bUget." Of course what she was telling me was that we needed to have a budget. We had a very meager income and we certainly needed a budget in order to make it financially and with God's help and the wise management of my husband we made it just fine.

Whether your income is large or small you do need to prepare a budget. You need to know the amount of money coming in and the amount of money going out. If you do not know how to prepare a budget there are many financial counselors available who offer their services as a ministry to the Lord. These financial counselors will help you to get your finances in order so that you will not be stressed out over bills that cannot be paid. And may I say here, as a personal testimony, that as a young couple we felt it important to pay tithes on our income first and then take care of our other obligations. We have been extremely blessed as a result of putting God first in our finances and by giving to missions and other worthy ministries. We have been blessed spiritually, physically and materially. Please keep this in mind; you can never go wrong obeying God's Word.

Give Me Some Money Too!

Another thing that is extremely important to remember is that each spouse should have some discretionary money that he or she feels free to spend. At the beginning of the marriage it may not be very much at all, but just a small amount makes a person feel a little independent. They tell us that money is power, and to a degree, maybe it is. When a spouse always has to ask for money, he or she probably feels somewhat powerless. It also has a tendency to make one feel like a small child who has to ask a parent for whatever he or she needs. The discretionary money for each spouse should be included in the budget and he or she should not have to give an account of how this money is spent. Just this simple act of kindness can make both spouses much happier with the money situation.

I know that it is often necessary for both spouses to be employed outside of the home. When both spouses are wage earners the income should be combined in your budget with each spouse feeling that he or she is being treated fairly. If one spouse is not a wage earner, he or she should be shown as much respect as the wage earner. Don't be guilty of making your spouse feel "less than" because he or she doesn't make any money or as much money as you. Value and respect the work done in the home and do your share by helping out with some of the household responsibilities. After all this is a marriage, the coming together of two individuals; this applies to your work and finances as well as in other areas of marriage.

Who Handles the Finances?

In marriage retreats I always ask couples this question, "Who should handle the finances in a marriage?" I am happy to say that over the years the answer has changed. For many years the answer was, "the man!" It seems that couples are now realizing that it is far safer and more beneficial financially for the spouse who has the most expertise in handling money, be the one to keep up with the family's finances. It may be that the wife is wiser in financial matters. This should not make her husband feel uncomfortable. He should be grateful that she is willing to take on this responsibility.

Whoever handles the finances, the husband or wife, should make his or her spouse aware of what is going on in this area. It is very important that husbands and wives sit down together and look at their financial situation. When a husband or wife is kept in the dark regarding finances he or she will probably be less understanding when it comes to the spending or saving of money. It always helps if occasionally both spouses go to grocery store together. It is amazing how much groceries cost! Unless you go to the store you have no idea that bread or any other item could be so expensive. Just be aware of these things so you won't gripe about what is being spent.

Prepare for the Future

The Bible does say that we are not to lay up treasures on this earth but at the same time we are told to be wise stewards of what God has given us. As a wise steward we are careful with our finances now so we will not be without when we get older. We prepare for the future by taking care of important money manners now. Again, there are wise counselors who can guide you in how to do this. Do not hesitate to ask for advice.

Proverbs 15:22
2 Plans fail for lack of counsel,
but with many advisers they succeed.

It is very sad when a spouse dies and the spouse who is left has no knowledge of income or indebtedness. Many times the living spouse is even clueless as to what insurance or investments they might have. Remember marriage is a partnership and both partners are investing so both should be aware of everything (finances included) that is going on. Talk with each other about where you are now financially and what your financial goals are for the future. When you do this there is less wrestling over money now and there will be less wrestling over money in your future. Whether you have little or much you are in this thing together, so as our grandchildren say, "you must share," your goals and dreams "until death you do part."

10

"NAGGER" – "NEEDLER" –"NESTLER"

First of all, I would like to talk to you ladies about the power you have in your home, but I am not going to leave you men out of this, so just hang on. Ladies, you have a lot of power. I can almost hear some of you saying, "I need to hear this." Take a look at ***Proverbs 14:1 "The wise woman builds her house, but with her own hands the foolish one tears hers down."*** I am sure that you would agree with me that a woman who can tear down or build up her house has "some kind" of power.

Let's begin by noting that the emotional climate in the home is created by the wife. Most of us have heard the saying that "if Mama ain't happy, ain't nobody happy." A wife, by her attitude and behavior will build up her house or tear it down. What power! What a challenge! In thinking of this challenge, it makes sense for any woman to occasionally do a little introspection, a personal check-up, to see if she is building her house or tearing it down.

We know that a wife does not physically tear down or build up her house. However, it is very possible for a wife to destroy the peace and harmony that should be in a healthy home and in doing this she is tearing her house down. On the other hand, a wife is just as capable of creating an atmosphere of peace and harmony which builds up her home. I also believe it is possible for a husband to destroy the peace and harmony in the home by his attitude and behavior.

In this chapter I want to look at three different ways of interacting which will lead to the building up or tearing down of a household. The first two are negative; the third one is positive. All three are presented in the form of a question and the answer given will determine whether you are building up or tearing down your household.

ARE YOU A "NAGGER"?

A "nagger finds fault incessantly." Here is my personal acronym for the word "nagger." If you are a "nagger," you are **Needlessly Agitating, Grating, and Grinding,** and **Ever Reminding.** Would you fit the description of a nagger? Would you say that you are agitating those around you by ever reminding them of what they should be doing? I can just about hear some of you saying, "I have to nag, or things will not get done."

Agitate, Grate and Grind

Count the times that your nagging has brought you the desired results; in reality nagging is useless, it does absolutely no good. It tears down the self esteem of the person who is being nagged and it angers and tears down the person doing the nagging. "You can never change anyone by direct action." This is a universal law that explains why nagging doesn't work. In other words, we try to change a person's behavior by telling him or her over and over (nagging) what we want them to do. You think if you keep on and on about something you would like to see changed that finally the message will get through and the person will change the behavior that is so frustrating to you. That is wishful thinking!

Nagging Can Become a Habit

Anyone, husbands or wives, can get into the habit of nagging when things are not done that they wish to see done. It seems that once we get in the habit of nagging it becomes a vicious cycle. We nag at someone to change and when they don't, we get angry and nag even more.

However, we can nag all we want to and it will not result in a permanent change of behavior. I say permanent change because sometimes a person will become so upset with the constant nagging that he or she will, in anger, change for the moment. This type of change usually doesn't last very long because it was made in the anger of the moment.

A relationship where one or both spouses are nagging is probably a relationship where there is very little nestling going on.

One Time Only

The most efficient way to get something done or bring about change in a person's behavior is to make a very specific request to the person one time and one time only. Make sure you were heard and understood so that there is no misunderstanding as to what you want your spouse or your child to do. If he or she fails to follow through on completing the task, don't nag, let the task go undone or do it yourself without complaining. Strive to develop a positive attitude about the whole situation. Many times the change in your attitude will bring about the results that your nagging could not do. But I do want to emphasize that this is not a guarantee that you will get the results that you really want. If you don't get the desired results, try something else, just do not nag!

ARE YOU A "NEEDLER"?

A "needler" incites action by repeated gibes. The acronym that I use for needler is **N**udging, **E**xpressing, **D**riving, **L**eading, **E**xploding, and **R**ebelling. Gibes pierce just like a needle. This sounds a little cruel doesn't it? I can just picture someone with a long needle giving a little gibe here and a little gibe there – Oh, that hurts! We don't think we could be that cruel, but in reality; most of us have given little gibes to our spouse to try and get what we want. We don't mean to hurt; we just want him or her to get with it, to get motivated, so we just give them a little gibe.

Expecting Too Much

Many wives and husbands create problems in their marriage because they want too much and expect too much, but instead of nagging they just needle their spouse to get what they want. To be honest, sometimes it is difficult to find the delicate balance between encouraging and needling. There are times we need to ask ourselves are we pushing too hard to get what we want or are we expecting more from our spouse than he or she is able to give.

Little Nudges

Needling can occur over many, and sometimes very simple, things. A wife may want her husband to make more money, or a husband may want his wife to dress differently; everyday things we would like to see change, as we see it, for the better. To get these expectations met we usually begin with a little nudge here and a little nudge there, needling just a little bit. But if the nudges don't work, we might start expressing, very vocally, how unhappy we are over the situation.

Expressing Sarcastically

Some spouses express their unhappiness with sarcastic gibes in order to incite the other person to action. Of course we should all know that sarcasm aimed at another person is very cruel and should never be a part of communication in a marriage, but it does happen. However, when all expressions of dissatisfaction or unhappiness fail to incite to action we begin to push a little harder.

Leader Then Driver

In pushing harder we can actually begin to drive our spouse. This is often done when one takes the role of a dominant leader who demands that certain goals should and must be met. When the wife becomes the leader or begins to drive her husband, she takes the role of a mother which can create havoc in a marriage. There was a time in our marriage that I assumed the role, (unknowingly) of mother, to my husband.

I was taking some college courses at a campus near the church my husband pastored at that time. Because I enjoy studying and because it was fun for me I thought it would be fun for my husband also. I kept needling him about taking some courses as a diversion from his pastoral duties. My husband told me several times that he would think about it but I kept needling until he finally agreed to go with me to the campus and sign up for one or two courses. Well, I am embarrassed to say that I almost took him by the hand to registration, and the day classes began I showed him the room where his class would be held. To make matters worse, I checked in on him to see how he was getting along. It is hard for me to believe that I could have been so unwise. Needless to say, he informed me shortly thereafter, that he needed a wife and lover, not a mother. This brought me to my senses and I shaped up and I have tried very hard never to assume the role of his mother and drive him to do something he really doesn't care to do. I enjoy being his wife and lover tooooo much!

Real Damage - Explosion

The next step in the art of "needling" is the exploding stage. When all else fails we will verbally explode when our expectations are not met. We taunt our spouse for not doing better, whether it is to lose weight, make more money, get a better job, or become the spiritual leader in the home.

Sometimes we will subconsciously compare our spouse with someone else and if our spouse doesn't measure up we may explode because we feel like we are being cheated and that life is not fair. Any explosion can create havoc and many times cause death; it can do the same in a marriage.

Rebellion by
Running or by Closing Down

An explosion can lead to the attitude "if he or she is not going to live up to my expectations then I will be better off making it on my own." Often when a couple reaches this point in their relationship they will not wrestle or nestle, they will just give up. The end result may well be that some will rebel and run away physically and some will run away emotionally; both are devastating.

Do your best not to be a "needler," it leads to a dead end. Remember there are better ways of getting your expectations met; become a "nestler."

ARE YOU A "NESTLER"

To nestle means to press closely and affectionately – to settle. Are you ready for the acronym for "nestler?" Here it is; **N**ourishing, **E**ncouraging, **S**oothing, **T**ouching, **L**eveling, **E**mpowering, and **R**emembering. This is the essence of marriage! To **NESTLE!!** There is nothing so beneficial to a marriage than to develop the habit of nestling. How beautiful to press in closely to our spouse; to press in emotionally, psychologically, spiritually, and physically. This is what God intended marriage to be; a relationship where we can feel settled in the love of our spouse.

Nourishing Brings Vitality

Good marriages do not just happen, they have to be nourished. Anything that is living needs nourishment in order to grow or it will die; the same is true of a marriage. Nourishing a marriage takes time and effort, something that we often forget, but it is absolutely necessary if a relationship is going to remain vital and alive. There are marriages that have lasted twenty, thirty, or even fifty years but they are not vital, they are what is known as devitalized or empty shell marriages. An empty shell marriage consists of two individuals sharing a house, but each going about his/her own way, sharing very little of himself/herself with the other. Marriage is meant to be more than that! Nourish your marriage and it will grow and stay vital.

Encourage One Another

One of the ways to nourish you marriage is by being an encourager. You become an encourager by looking for ways to show your spouse that you are proud of who he or she is and of his or her accomplishments. Don't be stingy with compliments – give them freely.

Wives, we are told that the three most important words for a man to hear are, "I respect you," just three little words, but so powerful. Let that husband know that you respect him. Husbands, we are also told that the three most important words for a wife to hear are, "I love you." Let me tell you, as a wife, I never tire of hearing my husband say those three little words! I know that some of you will say that you would rather show your spouse how much you respect him or how much you love her and doing that is certainly to be appreciated, but you also need to verbally state how you feel. Put those arms around him or her and give an encouraging hug and utter those "three important words!

Soothing

Life is hard and we all suffer the emotional cuts and bruises that happen as we go about living. People say things and do things that really hurt us. There is no way that we can avoid all of life's battles but having a spouse who holds us close when we are hurting is like having a soothing ointment placed on an open wound. As Christians we know that we have the Lord Jesus to help us when we are hurting and He does in wonderful ways. However there are times when we need another human being to hold us close to soothe our hurts.

We are like the little girl who, when she was so frightened at night, called her mother and told her how afraid she was. The mother assured her that Jesus was with her and that she need not be afraid. The little girl answered, "Mommy, I know that Jesus is with me, but tonight I want someone with skin on to hold me." There are times we need someone with skin on to hold us. When you come home all beaten down emotionally, it means so much to have a spouse who can gently hold you in his or her arms. When we are nestled in arms of love it helps to soothe our bruised egos and makes life's battles much easier to bear.

Touching

The power of touch cannot be overstated. The need for touching begins at the moment of birth and it never ceases until the day we die. There are many wonderful reports from the medical community that verify the power of touch in the healing of those who are sick and dying. In fact, we continue to learn about the power of touch in helping those who are emotionally and physically ill.

When I was in graduate school we looked at a study done on a number of babies, who, many years ago, had been placed in a foundling home. These babies were given enough food to survive but because there were so many of them and so few helpers the babies were not held or even touched very often. The greater percentage of these babies did not survive, not from lack of food, but from the lack of touch. This study made us even more aware that our physical and emotional well being is greatly affected by touch.

In the marriage relationship touch is just as powerful. I tell couples to touch constantly. When you pass through the room touch your spouse on the arm, head, or give a quick hug. Make some kind of body contact. As my husband and I ride down the road one of us will reach over and take the other's hand or maybe I'll reach over and rub his neck. These touches are little nestles that make us feel loved and they help keep us close.

A Negative Illustration

A negative illustration of the power of touch has to do with unresolved anger between a husband and wife. To illustrate, let's say that a couple has gone to bed still angry with each other over something they had been arguing about all day. May I interrupt our story to tell you that you definitely do not want to go to bed while you are still angry with your spouse.

To continue our illustration, we will say that the couple slept in the same bed, and we could safely assume that they made certain that they had no bodily contact. We could also assume that the husband slept way over on his side of the bed and his wife slept way over on her side of the bed because they did not even want their toes to touch. Why? They wanted to stay angry and they were afraid that if their toes touched it might have started something and one or both were so stubborn they wanted to fume a little longer.

Does this silly little scenario sound familiar? If it does, please learn quickly that it is much better to touch, resolve the situation, and go from the wrestling stage to the nestling stage. When you do this both of you can get a good night's sleep. Yes sir! Touch carries a powerful punch no matter how gentle the touch.

Leveling

A marriage relationship must have honesty. I believe in being honest and leveling with each other but sometimes we do not level for the right reason. It is easy to say we are just being honest when we tell our spouse something that might be upsetting to him or her. It may be that what we say is true but we need to examine our motive as to why we feel the need to level with our spouse at that particular moment. Are we leveling with him or her because we are angry or are we trying to get even because of some supposed or real hurt we might have suffered in the past? That is not a good justification for leveling. True leveling is done in love, at the right time and for the right reason. When we level <u>in</u> <u>love</u> it brings us closer together.

Empowering

We empower our spouse when we help him or her to recognize strengths and potentials within. To borrow a phrase from a very popular song "we become the wind beneath their wings." There is a thrill in helping someone we love to become all he or she is capable of becoming. I would like to share with you a definition of love that one of my under graduate professors, Dr. Gilbert, shared with his class:

Love is the abiding desire on the part of two (2) people to produce together the conditions under which each can be and express his or her real self. To produce together the intellectual soil and the emotional climate in which each can flourish far superior than what either could have achieved alone. It exists only when two people produce it.

I just love that definition and to me it illustrates perfectly what empowering means in a marriage relationship.

Remembering

Remember how you felt when you first knew that you were in love with your spouse. Remembering is especially helpful when you are discouraged in your marriage. It helps to sit down and remember all the good times you have had together and allow yourself to believe that good times will come again. Memory is a powerful tool when used for good. You should refrain from dredging up unpleasant memories but focus instead on the good things in your relationship.

I like to remember simple things like the first time my husband held my hand when we were dating. We often talk about this and other sweet memories we have of when we were dating and so much in love. When we keep the memories of these little simple things alive it strengthens our relationship and helps to keep us still so much in love. Don't let these kinds of memories in your love relationship die but keep them alive and share them with each other often.

We are at the end of this chapter so, are you a "Nagger," "Needler," or "Nestler? Your answer will probably be somewhat similar to mine, which is, I honestly try not to nag but sometimes I do needle a little bit. But I am happy to say that over the years I have learned to do a lot more nestling which has resulted in our relationship being almost, I said almost, perfect.

EPILOGUE

In concluding this book I would like to share with you a few things that my husband and I have been able to do that has helped us to nestle.

Laugh Together

We have spent a lot of time laughing with and, at times, good-naturedly laughing at each other. An incident that we thought was hilarious happened one evening when my husband and I had gone out to eat with friends and we were getting in the car to leave the restaurant. My husband, as usual, opened my door, waited until I got in and then closed my door. He then proceeded around the car to get in on the opposite side. As he was going around the back of the car, our friend, who was driving, did not realize that my husband was not in the car, so he started to drive off. I became so tickled over the situation that I could not say anything, but my poor husband was hollering and beating on the trunk of the car while our friend continued to drive away. Finally he heard my husband's cries and stopped the car. We all laughed so hard, my husband included, that we cried. My husband jokingly said that we did not have to hit him with a brick to make him know when he was not wanted. Of course, I hugged him and assured him that we could not do without him.

Silly Together

Once in a while it doesn't hurt to purposefully be silly, no matter how old you get. We do a lot of silly things to make life fun. Once when we were vacationing in Gatlinburg, Tennessee, we decided one night to be silly. On that particular night, after we had been watching the Country Music Awards on TV, we decided to get dressed and go out for pizza. "You Picked a Fine Time to Leave Me Lucile," was the song that had won all the awards that particular year. We made our way to the restaurant through a light rain. With an umbrella over our heads we skipped down the street singing together, rather loudly, "You Picked a Fine Time to Leave Me Lucile." We were acting very silly but we sure had a lot of fun.

Creating Simple Rituals

We have several little rituals that make us feel so comfortable and loved. A ritual that we really enjoy is one we usually observe every year. Several years ago we started going out to a restaurant for breakfast on Christmas Eve morning. We eat out quite a bit so that is not why we feel this time together is so special. It is special because it is our personal ritual and after all these years we still begin early in the holiday season talking about and looking forward to our special Christmas Eve breakfast. It makes us feel so warm and cozy; it is one of life's little comforts.

Crying Together

We are told that if we live long enough heartache will come to all of us. Several years ago my husband and I suffered something so heartbreaking that it is difficult to describe. We suffered the heartache of parents who have lost a child in death.

We have had three children but now we only have two that are still with us. The middle child, a little girl of ten, died as a result of a freakish accident. She was a joy to us as well as to many others. When the accident claimed her life we were absolutely devastated, and to be honest, I personally questioned God. It was a rough time in our marriage as well as in our family. But because we did have faith in God and because we had one another we made it through that very difficult time in our lives. Now as we stand by her small monument, we cry together and many times my husband takes me in his arms as we stand together remembering our little darling and how very much we loved her.

Heartaches will come, in some form, to your life but that is a time when you need to hold each other close and just nestle. These trying times can, if you will let them, draw you closer together and make your love for each other grow stronger.

Life is so precious and the marriage relationship can be so wonderful please don't waste your time wrestling, make up your mind to spend a lifetime holding your spouse affectionately close. **NESTLE – NESTLE - NESTLE**